The information contained in this book and on the related Web site is intended for reference only and is not intended as medical or professional advice. Information contained herein is designed to give you the tools to make informed decisions about your lifestyle and health. It should not be used as a substitute for any treatment that has been prescribed or recommended by your healthcare provider.

While the author is a healthcare professional, she expressly disclaims any responsibility for any effects occurring as a result of use of the suggestions or information herein. If you suspect you have a medical problem, it is imperative that you seek appropriate medical attention.

Health Angels
Phoenix, Arizona 85212


Pearls of Wellness: 52 Inspirations to Achieve
  a Peaceful Body, Mind, and Spirit
Printed in the United States


ISBN 9780981650708
Library of Congress 2008931470


Cover design by Laura Orsini/Words Made Easy

What if you were to receive a chance to live
a more joyful, fulfilling, passionate life — all because
you had discovered your body-mind-spirit connection?

Would you?

Please accept this gift that will enable you
discover for yourself the greatest gift of all —
pearls to help you achieve a higher state of wellness.

# Dedication

This book is dedicated to:


My family — Mom, Dad, Daniel, Michael,
Dara, and Alden — for your love


And to my friends and colleagues — for your support


And to all of the readers —
for following your path of personal growth

# In Loving Memory

Grandma Ruth Bank
1915-2001

and

Grandpa Mike Bank
1914-2008

# Acknowledgments

It is challenging to consider all the people who helped make this book possible, because these pearls come from a lifetime of interactions with family, friends, mentors, patients, and students.

The dedication of this book begins with my family. Mom, you are the most caring, amazing woman I know. Dad, thank you for standing behind me every step of the way. Grandpa, you are an inspiration to everyone you meet. Daniel and Michael, who could ask for better brothers? Dara, we may not be related by blood, but you a sister to me. Alden, this book would not exist without your love and support.

To my friends and colleagues, I thank you. You are an infinite source of wisdom and guidance. You have each touched my life and helped me grow. The administration of A.T. Still University has been incredibly supportive. Dr. McGovern, Dr. Magruder, Dr. Phelps, Dr. Wendel, and Dr. Danielsen, I am proud to be on your faculty. Mike, Emily, Bob, Tracy, Jamie, Michelle, Sheree, Linda, Cynde, and Nancy, I love working with you. What a team!

To the readers of this book, may love and light shine through you. And to my students, may your wings of compassion touch the hearts of your patients. Scott Johnson, thank you for your willingness to inspire others by sharing your story of living with cystic fibrosis.

A special thanks to the contributors to this book. Scott Bennett, you are a true healer because you connect with others on a deep soul level. Dara Holz, you inspire those around you to grow and rediscover the beauty in life. Alden Witte, you bring out the best in everyone, and guide them toward self-discovery. The three of you have an incredible combination of wisdom and warmth. Your contributions to this book are tremendous.

To my editors, you are amazing. Mom, you taught me how to write and have edited this book more times than I can count. I am so grateful. Dad and Susan Kavanaugh, thank you so very much for your editing expertise and supportive guidance. Laura Orsini, you have turned words on a page into an eloquent and beautiful book, and designed a gorgeous cover that pulls it all together.

Thank you.

# Contents

# Contents

# Foreword

The book you hold in your hands is a precious gem. It is as good, if not better, than such books as the *Book of Proverbs* and *Poor Richard's Almanac*. It is a classic, in both style and in substance.

This book contains a polished pearl of wisdom for each of the 52 weeks of the year. It could be read on Sunday nights to get you charged up for the week or on Monday mornings to begin your week with a treat. Whichever way you choose to incorporate it into your life, it will change that life.

Here, in a well-written, well-researched book, is a beautiful path to wellness. It is like your favorite herbal tea — it goes down with pleasure and is good for you.

Reading this book and implementing its principles will make you highly functional in body, sound of mind, and rich in spirit. These interactions will help you not only avoid sickness, but to be well and live healthy. Regularly accessing this information will allow you to treat your body holistically so you can achieve top performance in all areas.

Carry this book with you, and read its weekly message every day of each week; then repeat it again next year, and every year thereafter. Give a copy to your spouse, your best friend, and others in your life whom you wish well.

This book is the gift of a life well lived.

James J. McGovern, Ph.D.
Former President, A.T. Still University of Health Sciences

# Introduction

I was working with a small group of healthcare professional students in lab one day, trying to give them every *pearl* I could think of before they ventured off to see "real" patients. These were not just medical tidbits I wanted to share, but ways to really take care of a patient. I wanted the students to know how to speak to and connect with the whole person — not just address a sore throat or headache. The students were very involved in the conversation, jumping in with ideas and thoughts when they could, and looking frustrated when they didn't know the answer.

Afterward, one of them asked me if I had this information in a PowerPoint presentation format. I laughed. We gave so many PowerPoint lectures over the past year that the faculty had begun to use the phrase, "PowerPoint poisoning." The PowerPoint presentations covered the *science* of medicine. Our discussion that day was based on the practical pearls I had discovered through years of experience — truly, what I like to call the *art* of medicine. I jokingly told this student that I'd connect a jump-drive from my brain to his so I could download this knowledge to him.

This book, a mental jump-drive from my brain to yours, is written from a healthcare provider's perspective, but it is intended for anyone who is seeking personal wellness for a more fulfilling life through the body-mind-spirit connection.

I believe that much of disease stems from stress and failing to take care of oneself. When uncontrolled, stress is like a fertilizer that helps both physical and psychological symptoms grow.

After all, how can you expect your body, mind, and spirit to take good care of **you**, if you don't take care of **them**? This book begins with the concept of disease, and then leads into general information about stress and its effects on the body. Next, it dives into short sections that teach you how to deal with multiple levels of wellness, both psychological and physical.

Congratulations for reading this book and taking this small but very important step to begin taking control of your physical, mental, and spiritual wellness!

To your health and happiness —

*Laura*

# 1. Dis-ease

*A bodily disease which we look upon as whole and entire*
*within itself, may, after all, be but a symptom*
*of some ailment in the spiritual part.*
— **Nathaniel Hawthorne**

Take a look at the components of this word, "disease." The first portion, **dis**, means something negative, while **ease** means a state of comfort, peace, or rest. When **disease** is present, the body's natural state of ease has been disrupted, and an imbalance is present — too much of one thing, or not enough of something else.

or example, the body may contain too much cholesterol, leading to fatty buildup in the arteries. Or the thyroid could be under-producing (hypothyroidism), leading to a plethora of symptoms, such as weight gain, fatigue, or depression.

On a similar note, consider autoimmune disorders. These are conditions that cause the immune system to actually attack the body! Examples include rheumatoid arthritis, type 1 diabetes, and lupus. Many autoimmune diseases wax and wane in severity over time, and not surprisingly, they generally worsen during stressful times. Why does this happen? No one knows for sure. But if your mind and spirit are in a state of dis-ease, it becomes challenging for your body to maintain health or heal at its peak capacity.

The study of mind-body medicine is called psychoneuroimmunology. Scientifically speaking, this is the study of the nervous system, the endocrine (hormone) system, the immune system, and the implications of these linkages for physical health.

Unfortunately, a big challenge for both providers and patients alike is the fact that we really have a "sick" care system instead of a "health" care system. While this evolution is frustrating, the potential for change grows as more individuals continue to embrace a holistic approach. I believe Hippocrates was right on target in the sixth century B.C. when he said, "For this is the great error of our day, that the physicians separate the soul from the body."

Health is not simply the absence of disease – is a state of optimal physical, mental, social, and spiritual well-being. The condition of true health means taking care of oneself on multiple dimensions. This goes far beyond the traditional notion that healthy eating and exercising are the keys. While these offer a great start, they address only the body's physical needs.

Have you ever considered how stressors, drama, work frustrations, family difficulties, and sadness affect you? Do pessimism and fear predominate your thoughts? If so, it becomes easy to attract more negativity into your life. "Like attracts like" is a spiritual law of the universe. Negative thoughts, emotions, and stressors weaken the immune system, disabling the body's natural defense system and potentially allowing disease to enter.

On the flip side, consider the effect of affirmative thinking, surrounding yourself with loving and supportive people, working in a field you enjoy, giving generously to others, and taking time for yourself. These sorts of actions will strongly attract more positive energy into your life which, in turn, influences your health, attitude, outlook, and joyfulness. Again, "like attracts like," so healthy, vibrant, positive thoughts will permeate the body.

Understanding this concept is the foundation for optimizing health and wellness.

# 2. Stress - Today's Woolly Mammoth

*The time to relax is when you don't have time for it.*
— **Author Unknown**

In prehistoric days, dealing with stress was much simpler than it is today. If you were a caveman being chased by a woolly mammoth, your natural instinct would possibly be to fight back, but probably to run. Hence the term, "fight or flight" response. The act of running releases stress hormones such as adrenalin and cortisol, which are important for maintaining proper blood sugar levels, aiding the immune system, blood pressure

control, and physiological changes that protect the body. This innate process is designed to help us survive in dangerous situations.

In today's world, the woolly mammoth confronts us in the form of everyday situations like deadlines, family stress, an angry boss, and/or rush-hour traffic. Yet instead of running, we tend to plant ourselves in front of the computer or TV, or hold in our frustrations until the stress hormones build up to the point that we become fatigued or sick. Stress has psychological and physiological manifestations that disrupt our natural state of balance. This disruption often leads to dis-ease.

## Physical Manifestations of Stress

In the woolly mammoth example, the endorphins released by the body act as a natural painkiller. Additionally, the dangerous situation does not allow  time to deal with the discomfort because it is much more important just to stay alive. When we feel threatened, the brain's alarm system is instantly triggered, signaling the body to send a flood of neurochemistry cascading throughout our bloodstream and nerve fibers:

- Our pupils dilate, allowing better vision, either in light or in darkness.
- Our heart rate increases, allowing more blood to flow through the body; simultaneously, the blood vessels constrict, minimizing potential blood loss.
- Our respiration rate rises to increase the oxygenation of the blood.
- Blood is diverted to the body parts that most need it, such as the muscles, rather than the digestive system or kidneys.
- Sweating increases to cool the body down and "goose bumps" may arise to increase sensitivity — though they are less helpful in humans than, say, porcupines, which have quills they deploy when threatened.

## *Psychological Manifestations of Stress*

Psychological responses to stress include feeling anxious, excitable, and irritable. Sweaty palms and a pounding heart make it difficult to appear calm and perform technical skills. When our primary attention is on survival, our focus is diverted from thinking at higher levels, so it's difficult to perform at peak intellect. Long-term stress can often lead to general symptoms such as malaise and difficulty with concentration.

Dr. Hans Selye (1907-1982) first compared short-term reactions to stress with long-term reactions to stress, or general adaptation syndrome:

**Stage 1**  The fight-or-flight response, as described above.

**Stage 2**  Resistance, also called the stage of adaptation. As stress continues to build in intensity, the body adapts. For example, the body may become used to getting less sleep each night while trying to balance a demanding job and a newborn baby.

**Stage 3** Exhaustion. At this point, the stress has continued over time and reached a level where the body can no longer effectively resist it.

Most healthcare providers would agree that stress can contribute to virtually any physical problem, such as heart disease, back pain, depression, and diabetes. The most common time for a heart attack to occur is on Monday mornings, which correlates with the start of the workweek for most people.

Even minor illnesses are often stress related. Think about it: If you are stressed, your body is not functioning at its peak level. Therefore, your immune system is functioning at a suboptimal level. So it's much easier to catch a cold, the flu, or worse. Some studies show that as many as 90 percent of all visits to primary care physicians are directly or indirectly related to stress.

## Eustress vs. Distress

There are two categories of stress, distress and eustress. Distress is the negative form that first comes to mind when you hear the word "stress." Eustress, on the other hand, is good stress. It's the type of stress that accompanies positive events, like planning a wedding or starting a new job. Eustress keeps us on our toes and vital. It helps us achieve goals, such as meeting a deadline. Keep in mind that the effect of a given stressor is difficult to identify, especially differentiating between eustress and distress, because each affects people differently. Riding a roller coaster might be a high for one person, but terrifying for another. Regardless, both types of stress can lead to profound effects on the body's physiology and biochemistry.

Recognizing eustress is helpful because it better allows us to cope as situations arise. For example, let's say you are planning a family vacation and become frustrated while trying to work out some of the details. You mention this to a coworker or spouse, who doesn't understand why it's causing you stress. "It's a vacation," they say, "and it is supposed to be fun." Sure, it's fun. But planning the details can also be very stressful. Hence the term eustress, which means "good stress." The recognition that ***happy events can also*** *be stressful events* can offer a new perspective, beyond the traditional inference that all stress is bad.

However, the body recognizes only that a change from its normal stimulus patterns has occurred; it does not distinguish whether the source of the stress is positive or negative. The designation of eustress or distress lies strictly in the mind of the person experiencing the stress, as the body reacts to good and bad stress in the same manner.

## Men and Women Handle Stress Differently

Many factors affect how an individual reacts to stress. These include gender, health status, age, race, education, culture and socioeconomic status. For example, men and women tend to react to stress differently. Until the mid-1990s, studies of the sympathetic nervous system or the "fight-or-flight" response focused primarily on men. This was rationalized by concerns about potential inconsistencies associated with women's menstrual cycles. From a primal survival standpoint, a fight-or-flight response makes sense for men, who were hunting and gathering. But what about pregnant women or those tending to their young? They were naturally in a protective mode and therefore hypersensitive to potential dangers.

Dr. Shelley Taylor and colleagues developed a model called *"tend and befriend"* that adds another dimension to the stress response. This model helps describe how females more commonly respond to stress, and are likely influenced by a female reproductive hormone called oxytocin. "Tending" refers to the woman's need to protect and nurture her children during stressful situations. "Befriending" relates to a woman's tendency to reach out to her community and friends for social networking and emotional support.

Think about the last time *you* went through a difficult situation. Did you reach out to others? Did you ask for help? Did talking about it help you explore options and work through the issue? If this was your approach, how would it compare to holding in the stress and processing everything by yourself? Were you physically affected by the situation, perhaps experiencing headaches, fatigue, or tight muscles?

Recognizing that stress plays such a tremendous role in our physical and mental well-being is the first step. Next, we must do something about it. Most of us are familiar with the usual "de-stressors." Eating right, exercising, getting proper sleep, etc. But what if you switch to healthier foods, but do not like the way they taste? What if you exercise because you are supposed to, but you don't enjoy it? Rather than helping you de-stress, these "healthy" activities further compound your already high stress levels!

Stress takes a huge toll on the body and can unfortunately weaken your immune system, opening the door for dis-ease. This book contains thought-provoking ideas, suggestions, and pearls to guide your journey toward total wellness through a peaceful body, mind, and spirit.

# 3. The Mind-Body Connection

*Health is a state of complete physical, mental, and social well-being,
and not merely the absence of disease or infirmity.*
**— World Health Organization**

If the human body is a complex machine, then the human brain
is one of the most intricate and enigmatic engines the body
contains. We know many scientific facts about the brain's
structure and patterns, but very little about its emotional
components.

We undoubtedly live in an age of technological
advancement and scientific discoveries, yet we still
have limited theories and facts about
how the mind affects the body, and
vice versa. The two are clearly
connected; however, it seems that the
intricacies of their interactions and
the ways the body can provide a
window into the operation of the mind
have been overlooked.

Our bodies are literal storehouses of
muscle memory and emotional memory. This
is beneficial and life preserving in some instances, but damaging in
others. Like all defenses, the initial response is one of self
preservation, but the question is: *"At what stage does a defense become
an encumbering, heavy suitcase one can never put down?"*

Some examples of ways muscle memory can serve us well are the
practice of dance, martial arts, sports, playing musical instruments,
or any kind of kinetic movement where our muscles hold the feeling
of the movement our brain has instructed them to perform. These
activities become part of our "muscle memory." Over time, our
bodies can shift, change, strengthen, increase in flexibility, and
become more adept as our brains become more efficient at
connecting the synapses. Because the pattern of activity has been

established in our brains and implemented by our bodies, we are able to accomplish the task at hand with greater efficiency and consistency.

We feel pride when we accomplish a new yoga move, slam dunk, or master vibrato on an instrument. We feel a sense of accomplishment when we achieve the connection between what we want to do and what we actually can do. Our capacity to store knowledge and ability to build on it in our minds and bodies is truly remarkable. Yet all the good things that can be achieved with muscle memory and collective brain activity can, unfortunately, have a flip side. These also can manifest in the form of trauma, fear, and repressed emotions that can find their way into our bodies and become a real pain in the neck — literally!

So what happens when we fall repeatedly, literally or metaphorically? Instead of being able to brush it off and get back on the horse, back on our feet, back to trusting and loving those around us, we can have a tendency to become more rigid, more guarded, more calculated with our movements, feeling less free, and emotionally and physically wounded.

Psychologist Dara Holz describes her experience with the mind-body connection:

> In my line of work — first as a certified massage therapist and later as a psychotherapist — I have noted a remarkable link between our bodies and minds and how we store stress, trauma, and emotions in both. I believe, and I am just one of many, that "talk therapy" or "massage therapy" can each be powerful alone — but together they are tremendously beneficial. (Just to clarify — for boundary issues — the two forms of therapy should not be provided by the same person. As a psychotherapist, I now always refer the patient out if they are interested in body work.)
>
> There is a theory that our emotional traumas are repressed and literally stored in different parts of our bodies. As a massage therapist, I combined Shiatsu, which is based on Chinese medicine, and deep tissue massage. I noted that when people

wanted to talk during the massage (although most preferred to enjoy the massage experience silently), their bodies released more fully.

Some people presented with "impenetrable" bodies — meaning that I could have literally stood on them and I wouldn't have been able to access their deep muscles. Their bodies seemed to be surrounded by shields of armor, only it was more like a wall than a healthy barrier — for I got the impression that if nothing bad was being let in, nothing bad was being let out, either. Their bodies felt toxic, and dense with the debris of anger, sadness, and mistrust. This is when I decided to attend graduate school to study psychology and further my exploration of the connection between the body and mind.

I am currently a therapist at a domestic violence shelter for women and children, and I see first-hand how the combination of fear, mistrust, and years of abuse and trauma insidiously enter not only my clients' psyches, but also their bodies, affecting their faces which tend to be hauntingly guarded. It takes a while for these women to trust me, and when they do choose to share some of the chaos of their lives with me, I see why they have acquired the "tough" facades, the blank and hollow looks, the guarded minds that remind me of the guarded bodies I used to massage. These women have endured years of physical, mental, and spiritual abuse. They have internalized it, repressed it, and locked it into their depths. Their fear and anger are palpable, and I note that their bodies are neglected — made either too thin or too large in the hope that no one will notice them. The mind-body connection is there in the room, like a third person watching silently but occupying a lot of space. The trauma is there.

But we make progress: we talk, we explore, we process, and I see subtle shifts. Releases such as crying and laughing occur. Empowering thoughts enter their minds and become reinforced when they aren't constantly shattered. I encourage them to move — to "get it out" so that the pain can release and exit the body. I suggest they walk or dance, anything to move the body and explore the places they are stuck so they can begin the healing process of ridding the physical body of stored negative emotions.

*I believe that by processing their emotions mentally, they will become more free physically. By the same token, movement will release stagnant cesspools of trauma and pain. The mind and body are a powerful duo, and it takes courage and time to regain the strength to heal in both areas. But we are strong, and we possess an innate body wisdom that, if we listen to it, will help us find health on multiple levels.*

*I ask my clients to pay attention to their feelings, both physical and mental, and to go at their own pace. Sometimes people tell me about their favorite breakfast foods, and other times they are willing to share the depths of their anguish. All is beneficial for the healing process. The name of the game, I tell them, is to begin listening to what their minds and bodies are whispering, singing, and screaming. I believe the human body and mind together can triumph over severe adversity. I believe that releasing emotions is a multilayered, complex process that is tangible and yet ephemeral at the same time. No wonder the mind-body connection is so under-understood.*

# 4. Religion and Spirituality

*The ego looks for peace ~ the spirit rests in it*
*The ego looks for love ~ the spirit gives it freely*
*The ego is in constant search for happiness ~ the spirit is absorbed in joy*
*The ego looks for control ~ the spirit is totally free*
*The ego looks for longevity ~ the spirit is immortal*
*The ego accumulates information ~ the spirit is Supreme Wisdom*
*The ego is limited by space and time ~ the spirit is boundless*
*The ego is only a player in a show ~ the spirit is life itself*
*The ego is false ~ the spirit is real*
*The ego wants more and more ~ the spirit has it all!*
— **Martin Broffman**

Religion can be a wonderful, nurturing reminder of our spiritual nature. If you have found a religion or spiritual practice that works for you, that is wonderful news. Does it leave you feeling fulfilled? Are you free to question yourself, your God, your universe? This type of freedom is important in your faith walk, regardless of which path you choose to follow. Questioning will lead you in your spiritual growth because it leads to a deeper understanding.

Take care not to allow your family members or others to insist that their religion is the right one for you. Only you can know *your* truth and what speaks to your heart. Following someone else's preference often leads to frustration and resentment.

There's an important distinction to be made when considering religion and spirituality. Spirituality is the way people strive to find meaning and purpose in their lives; religion is one avenue through which people may express their individual spirituality. Find a religion or spiritual practice that works for you, but remember it's okay to explore. The actual process of determining what is right for you will lead you to a higher path.

Do you feel more connected on top of a mountain or walking on a sandy beach, as compared to a traditional house of worship? God is everywhere — perhaps found in the smile of an infant or in a beautiful field of sunflowers. Just look around. Find the spiritual home that connects you to your higher self — your inspiration — whatever that may look like for you.

# 5. What Is Your Heart's Desire?

*Your imagination is your preview of life's coming attractions.*
— **Albert Einstein**

I went out to lunch one day with a group of women from work to our favorite gourmet hamburger restaurant. We made our usual rule that we were not allowed to discuss work related issues. (It's amazing how often we broke that rule!)

Out of the blue, one of my coworkers asked us to consider the following question: ***What are the things you want to do before you die?***

We went around the table, one by one, each stating the things that were most important to us. Universally, we listed travel. But beyond that, our answers varied tremendously as we named things from seeing *Phantom of the Opera* on Broadway to learning how to sail. We learned a lot about each other that day, and this single conversation had a tremendous impact on all our lives.

So this is my challenge to you: Write down *YOUR* list. What do you want to do during your remaining time on this planet? There are no right or wrong answers. Your list can range from simple acts you can do tomorrow to a grand vision that involves years of planning. The list could have ten things or a hundred . . . and, of course, make sure to leave room for additions.

As you begin to act on this list, you may want to start with an item that will allow you to experience a change in your outlook by doing something you really want to do. Starting with something meaningful will teach you that it's okay to give yourself permission to dream and act upon these desires.

Lastly, schedule a lunch date with your friends and ask them the same question. You might be amazed at what you learn about them, and how much you will truly inspire them to clarify their own dreams.

# 6. Plan a Date ... With Yourself

*It is essential to our well-being, and to our lives,
that we play and enjoy life. Every single day,
do something that makes your heart sing.*
— **Marcia Wieder**

This one sounds a little strange, doesn't it? Isn't a date supposed to involve another person? Let me back up a bit and provide an example.

In her book, *The Artist's Way: A Spiritual Path to Higher Creativity*, Julia Cameron assigns a regular task of planning a date, alone, for several hours each week. The date is something just for you — no one else is invited (though it's okay if other people happen to be at your destination).

While Cameron's book may be used as a creativity and spiritual guide for the solo reader, it is actually designed to be a group experience. Not the reading itself, but weekly group discussions of

the chapters and the accompanying exercises. During these meetings, the group members speak about their life journeys and spiritual growth. Among other topics, folks often discuss what they do for their weekly "dates." Most mention things like their favorite artistic venues, playing a musical instrument, or taking time out to see a much-anticipated movie. I was once invited to one of these group meetings where I met a spunky, 75-year-old woman named Ann.

Ann had heard in the news about "The Gates," Christo and Jeanne-Claude's grand-scale artistic creation, temporarily exhibited in New

York's Central Park. The artwork contained 7,503 gates, each 16 feet tall, spread over 23 miles of walkways. Orange-colored fabrics were suspended from each gate, flowing freely in the wind and hovering about seven feet above the ground.

When Ann heard about this massive and unusual work of art, she hopped on a train from North Carolina and went to see it for herself. She had an amazing, carefree experience strolling beneath the fabric art. Needless to say, her story was the highlight of that week's *Artist Way* group meeting! *Carpe diem.*

# 7. Be Selfish...Sometimes

*Learn to enjoy every minute of your life. Be happy now.*
*Don't wait for something outside of yourself to make you*
*happy in the future. Think how really precious is the time you*
*have to spend, whether it's at work or with your family.*
*Every minute should be enjoyed and savored.*
**— Earl Nightingale**

Wow, this one sounds crazy, huh? First a date with myself
— now this! Trust me — it's a good idea.

Let's make a general assumption that you have a lot of
responsibilities . . . to your family, your job, and your friends to
name only a few. Given these demands, chances are good that you

put everyone else's
needs before your
own. What
eventually happens
is that you feel run
down, and it
becomes difficult to
continue to give,
give, and give more
still, because you
have no reserves
left for yourself. So
if you take time to
occasionally put yourself first, those surrounding you will ultimately
benefit.

Recently a friend shared with me that when she was a child, her dad
always told her to be selfish 51 percent of the time. My mind
immediately inferred a negative connotation of the word selfish
before she explained further.

Selfish, in her family, meant taking care of oneself. They described it
as, "Doing what you need to do for you. Allowing yourself to have
fun, enjoy the little pleasures, and taking some alone time when
needed."

When we *don't* do this, we have a tendency to resent those around us when they take "me" time. We often find ourselves feeling fatigued and stressed because our entire lives revolve around others. When we *do* take time for ourselves, we feel refreshed and alive. So while it may seem like one more thing to add to an already busy schedule, taking some time for ourselves is one of the best things we can do, both for us and for those around us.

Have you ever had a really busy day at work where you just kept pushing through, not even taking a break for lunch? Often, after hours and hours of intense concentration, you reach a breaking point where it is difficult, if not impossible, to focus any longer. I find that taking the time to get out of the office to breathe in some fresh air and nourish my body with healthy food makes a huge difference in my productivity for the rest of the day. It's like hitting a reset button on my work.

Sometimes being selfish can take the form of being *selfless*. Have you ever taken an evening stroll through a beautiful park, only to be disgusted that someone has thrown a soda can or other trash on the ground, rather than using a trash bin? My suggestion is that you avoid creating mental garbage by allowing any physical trash you might encounter to bring you down. Instead of being frustrated at other people for littering, just pick it up. You will feel even better about yourself because you are making a contribution to the beauty around you.

# 8. Mix It Up

*You and I are essentially infinite choice-makers.*
*In every moment of our existence, we are in that field*
*of all possibilities where we have access to an infinity of choices.*
— **Deepak Chopra**

D o you find yourself reliving each day like the main character in the movie, *Groundhog Day*? For those who might not have seen it, the movie is about a weatherman (portrayed by Bill Murray) who is reporting on what he regards as the most dreaded day of the year, Groundhog Day. There's a long-held superstition that one famous groundhog in Punxsutawney, Pennsylvania (who just happens to be named Punxsutawney Phil) determines whether winter will soon end or continue for six more weeks. Phil's prediction depends on whether or not his shadow is visible on the second day of February, every year.

In the film, Bill Murray's character gets through this loathsome day, only to wake up the next morning to find himself reliving the exact same day. And it happens again and again, one day after another after another. No matter what he does — and he tries some pretty dramatic things — he is stuck, and it seems he will never escape living the rest of eternity in this rut. His process is interesting because, over time, he begins to realize what's important in his life. He experiences an awakening about his own life, and also about those around him.

The weatherman is so stuck in a pattern that he is not really awake to life. That's probably N-E-V-E-R happened to you, has it? The thing is, living unconsciously can be useful, because it saves us energy in that we don't have to consciously think about what to do every day. If we didn't have any patterns at all, getting through each day might be like having perpetual amnesia . . . needing to continually re-learn every activity.

But there's a difference between unconscious habits that serve us, and essentially sleepwalking through life. If you find yourself taking time to examine your life and you discover that it's uneventful or boring, try mixing things up a bit to begin the process of awakening.

Consciously changing is a great cure when you find yourself in a rut! Humans have hundreds, probably thousands, of patterns they follow each day. Just choosing to examine your patterns is a huge first step. It's even more effective to recognize how entrenched you may be in those patterns when you attempt to change them. Start simply. Try getting out of bed on the opposite side, brushing your teeth with your non-dominant hand, putting your jeans on starting with the alternate leg, taking a different route to work, connecting with an old friend who has been on your mind lately, or rearranging your furniture. Do anything that gets you out of your routine to make you feel something new and alive!

At times, it may be difficult to get away from the norm, yet if you consider it honestly, you may find this frustration is really a resistance to the waking process. Think about where you are stuck, and see if you can turn your resistance into a challenge. It's critical that you don't allow your mind to come up with excuses for avoiding this process.

You have a choice: you can stay in your old patterns or make strides toward expansion and growth. Be creative — as the famous Albert Einstein quote says, "We can't solve problems by using the same kind of thinking we used when we created them." Becoming more conscious is your goal. You wouldn't be reading this book if you were not ready for change and growth.

# 9. The Way of the Dog

*Live your life each day as you would climb a mountain.*
*An occasional glance toward the summit keeps the goal*
*in mind, but many beautiful scenes are to be observed*
*from each new vantage point. Climb slowly, steadily, enjoying*
*each passing moment; and the view from the summit*
*will serve as a fitting climax for the journey.*
**— Harold V. Melchert**

Perhaps the secret to seizing the day is that we need to be more like our dogs. I don't know about you, but I've occasionally declared "Dumb dog," about my lovable canine. But . . . hmm . . . are they really all that dumb? Dogs always seem to be happy, have low stress levels, and live life to the fullest. They greet their loved ones at the door every day, and demonstrate their affection openly and lovingly. When you think about it, they are always totally in the moment. Maybe we should use them as our role models, and try to be more present to our surroundings.

I recently visited a trendy vegan restaurant in Los Angeles. At first, the waitress appeared quite impressive when she took our entire order without writing it down. When we waited for quite some time without the food arriving, my confidence in her abilities dropped. "They lost your ticket in the kitchen," she explained, after asking us to repeat our order. But her presence, or lack thereof, told me otherwise. She spoke in auto-pilot language. Before finishing talking to us, she had already mentally moved on to her next table. Simple proof of this mental absence was her lack of eye contact.

Being present is essential. Since yesterday is gone and tomorrow never gets here, all we have is now. It's like a gift, and that's why they call it the "present." Hitting the auto-pilot switch is easy, simply going through the motions with all of our attention focused on what will happen next. My challenge to you is to be present in every moment.

Face-to-face communication is a great way to practice being fully present. Speaking with someone is a basic level of communication. The additional dimension of direct eye contact makes for a more meaningful connection. To maximize the experience, picture the outcome beforehand.

For example, let's say that you would like a friend to hand you a pen. Imagine your friend happily handing you the pen before you ever ask for it. It might not work the first time you try it, but as you practice, you may be surprised to find that you can influence the outcome just by imagining it ahead of time. While influencing someone to hand you a pen probably seems like an elementary task, it is a great tool to use as an experiment so that you can move on to bigger intentions.

As you become more confident in this technique, reaching for higher goals will be much easier. Let's take another example. If you are requesting a promotion at work, picture your boss gladly saying yes beforehand. Using all these modalities — language, eye contact, and visualization — will promote more effective communication.

Using these techniques will also help you to stay present, and being present is a beautiful gift you can give to both yourself and those around you. So go ahead, spend some time learning from a dog. They have a lot to teach us about living in the moment and loving life!

# 10. Soaring Seagull

*He who trims himself to suit everyone*
*will soon whittle himself away."*
— **Raymond Hull**

In the 1970s, Richard Bach wrote a very popular book about a misfit bird, called *Jonathan Livingston Seagull*. Instead of fighting for food with the rest of the flock, day after day, he followed his dream to learn how to soar across the skies. This led to his being labeled an outcast, and he was banned from the flock. The estrangement, while difficult, was necessary, because through it, the doors for his spiritual growth opened. Eventually, he returned to the flock to scope out other young seagulls who wanted more out of life.

The beauty and art of this seagull's flight is a great analogy for life. We can drudge through work and life, feeling miserable each day. Or, we can discover our passion and pursue it! Why wait for an external event to make us happy? Happiness is a state of mind, rather than a reflection of our circumstances.

One obstacle in this often-difficult process of self-determination is learning to divest ourselves of the opinions of others. Wanting to be accepted is natural. But what good does it really do to spend your life pleasing everyone else? Rather than doing what's best for others, focus on your own reality.

The good news is that being different is gradually becoming much more acceptable amid this "melting pot" in which we live. Following your heart and doing what is best for you will ultimately allow you become far more accepted by others. Don't be a phony and try to be just like everyone else simply to fit in. This is guaranteed to lead to misery because you are not being YOU.

What's more, our society doesn't need any more cultural clones. We do need you to explore who you are and why you are on this planet. Your existence is not an accident! Discovering your passion and living your purpose is the key. And the best news? You can do it while staying true to your own heart.

# 11. Have the "Best Day Ever"

*The concept of total wellness recognizes that our every thought, word, and behavior affects our greater health and well-being. And we, in turn, are affected not only emotionally but also physically and spiritually.*

**— Greg Anderson**

Have you ever noticed that when something good happens at the start of your day, it puts you in a good mood that lasts the whole day? Somehow, more good things tend to happen, and the day just keeps getting better and better!

Unfortunately, you may also have noticed the opposite. Perhaps you can't find your keys as you're running late for an important meeting. Then, after getting stuck in traffic, you make it to the office, but the bomb drops as you walk through the door. Before you know it, the whole day has become a disaster, as one bad/frustrating/challenging thing happens after the next.

Positive or negative, your mood and attitude tend to stay with you. But remember, you can control this! Pay attention to how you're feeling and what you're thinking — and if it's anything but positive, consciously break the cycle. Find the good in every situation, in the world around you, in life, and keep that as your focus. This may be challenging at first — but if you practice, you will get better at it. Wondering what good thing you could possibly focus on in  the midst of a rotten day? One great option is to focus on all the things for which you are grateful. You can do this in your head, or better yet, write them out, leaving room for frequent additions. This is a great tool to keep on hand so that you can read and add to it whenever you need a pick-me-up.

Another fantastic tool is to remember and mentally re-experience the highlights of your life. When were you incredibly joyful? What times of your life were the most amazing? Relive these moments in your mind. A powerful aspect of this technique is to go beyond simply thinking about these great moments to actually feeling the emotions you experienced at those times.

I remember once seeing a sign hanging on an office door that read, "Good morning, let the stress begin!" Wow, what an invitation to start the day on the wrong foot. Ask and ye shall receive. What would happen if, instead of believing that the world and universe are conspiring against you, you believed they were working *FOR* you? They do. Expect things to go your way, and your days to run smoothly. And when the inevitable doubts creep into your mind, visualize yourself being an excellent troubleshooter so that no problem is too much to handle and nothing can affect your positive outlook.

In 1973, psychologist Phillip Brickman conducted a study where he examined the happiness of those who had won a lottery, compared to those who had become quadriplegics. Over time, both sets of subjects returned to the same level of happiness they had experienced prior to their lottery winning or their accidents. This study is quite eye-opening because it reminds us that our happiness must come from within. There's no justification for the thought, "I'll be happy when . . ." because you could spend your whole life saying this and never get to the "when." Instead of waiting, why not make life as incredible as possible right now? This is determined by your attitude, not your circumstances!

What you believe in — what you make your reality — will come true. If you don't believe you are capable of finding happiness, you will experience despair, anger, resentment, or resignation. Instead, why not vow to have the best day ever? Try it. From your first thought in the morning and throughout the rest of your day, tell yourself again and again, "I am having the best day ever!"

# 12. Positive Language Only

*If you think you can do a thing*
*or think you can't do a thing, you're right*
**— Henry Ford**

I received as a gift a cute little sign that summarized the Australian philosophy, "No worries, mate." While looking for the perfect place to hang it, I was gently reminded of the message. You see, your subconscious has a hard time comprehending negative language, such as "no" or "not."

When you see a sign that says, "No worries, mate," your body actually interprets it as "Worries, mate."

Along the same lines, you probably want to avoid giving your children commands like "Don't slam the door!" because the child's subconscious hears, "Slam the door!" Instead, try, "Please close the door gently."

Think about other common phrases we tell ourselves:

"A moment on the lips means forever on the hips."

"He's going to give me a heart attack."

"I have a bad memory."

"I get sick every winter."

"I'm getting old."

When you say these things, you are correct! Your body internalizes these statements as truth.

When negative thoughts arise, you can turn them around into specific positive thoughts. Positive thoughts are much more powerful; learning to use them can quickly make an impactful difference in your life.

Begin your affirmation with an "I am" statement. Then use a word such as *ecstatic, thrilled, happy, blessed,* or *grateful.* Conclude the sentence with a specific descriptor. Keeping it short and easy to remember is important. Also, it must be believable to you, so think big, yet attainable.

Remember to keep your language positive. State what you want, not what you don't want. For example, "I don't want to be fat" is interpreted by your mind, the body's delivery mechanism, as "I want to be fat." So instead, try something like, "I'm so grateful for my thin, healthy body." Saying and internalizing this statement will physically and mentally prepare you to make healthier choices so you can begin to live the affirmation.

When making affirmations, also be aware of a very human tendency to hope and wish for things in the future. By doing this, things tend to STAY in the future. That's why affirmations work best when stated in the present tense, or with a specific timeline attached to them. For example, instead of hoping for a promotion, you can make an affirmation implying that it's already happened. Declaring and believing such a strong and specific statement creates a link between what you believe on the inside versus what's happening on the outside. The universe then aligns itself toward harmony by turning your beliefs into reality.

One last tip: Don't just say and believe your affirmations. FEEL them. Go inside your body and experience them. Celebrate the feelings that arise. Affirmations are much more powerful when accompanied by joyful, powerful feelings.

EXAMPLES

**Negative:**    I am worried that my medical tests will show cancer.

**Positive:**    I am so thankful for my healthy body and its natural ability to heal itself.

~~~

**Negative:**    It will be impossible to meet my sales quota for this month.

**Positive:**    I am thrilled to easily exceed my sales goals for this month by more than 150%.

~~~

**Negative:**    My house will never sell.

**Positive:**    I am ecstatic that my house will sell quickly and easily on or before (insert date here).

~~~

**Negative:**    I'm so bad with directions.

**Positive:**    I'm so grateful that I always find my way easily.

# 13. What the Bleep? Water

*Balance, power, and non-resistance are
lifelong lessons taught by water.*

**— Alden Witte**

Japanese scientist Dr. Masaru Emoto has performed thousands of experiments with water. In his book, *The Secret Life of Water*, and *What the Bleep Do We Know!?*, a movie about quantum physics, Emoto demonstrates how energy — including thoughts and words — affects everything, both internally and externally. The experiments were simple. He labeled samples of water with both positive and negative words, such as "love" or "hate." Later, he examined frozen water crystals from the various samples under a microscope and photographed the images he saw.

The microscope images revealed beautiful, brilliant crystals from the water exposed to positive words, music, or thoughts. Conversely, the water exposed to negative words, music, or thoughts revealed dull, dirty-looking, asymmetrical, jagged, and incomplete crystals.

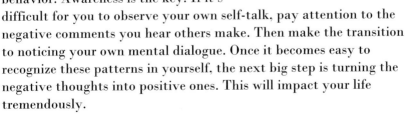

Consider the fact that the human body is comprised mostly of water. When we say positive or negative things to ourselves and those around us, what is the effect on our bodies? How great is the impact of our thoughts and words?

Noticing our negative thinking is a positive first step in changing our behavior. Awareness is the key. If it's difficult for you to observe your own self-talk, pay attention to the negative comments you hear others make. Then make the transition to noticing your own mental dialogue. Once it becomes easy to recognize these patterns in yourself, the next big step is turning the negative thoughts into positive ones. This will impact your life tremendously.

We deserve to treat ourselves — and be treated by others — with love, joy, kindness, and respect. So it's crucial to pay attention to our thoughts, words, and actions to make sure they are as positive as possible.

# 14. Time for a Change?

*If you keep on doing what you've always done,*
*you'll keep on getting what you've always gotten.*
**— W. L. Bateman**

It takes about a month to change a habit. If there is a change you've been wanting to make, but you've been hesitant to get started for some reason — maybe exercising more or eating healthier foods — challenge yourself to commit for just one month. You don't have to promise a lifetime of change . . . just 30 days. You will likely find that at the end of the month, this new behavior is no longer such a struggle. At that point, you can assess

whether it is a life change you are willing to commit to in the long run. Is the effort worth the potential benefit?

One way of easing into this new behavior is by finding substitutes that work for you. If your goal is to eat healthier, but you love pastries in the morning, think of something else that is tasty, yet healthy. How about making a smoothie with your favorite fruits? Maybe an egg white omelet with your favorite veggies? Or light yogurt with fruit and granola? Another way to approach it is by making the substitutions two or three times a week to begin with. If, however, you feel you cannot do without the pastries, what can you do for the rest of your day to eat healthier?

One great way to motivate yourself for change is to surround yourself with people who inspire you and who have already attained your goals. For example, if your goal is to be financially stable, do you want to surround yourself with people who are struggling financially? Of course not! Spend your time with and learn from people who are already stable. Think about the five people you are closest to; chances are good that your income is about the average of those five.

Or if you are trying to get in shape but having a difficult time motivating yourself to use the weight machines and cardiovascular equipment at the gym, take group classes instead. Having a dedicated instructor and connecting with others who also want to get in shape can be a great inspiration. Most importantly, have fun with it!

Many people hesitate to work out with others because they are overweight or out of shape. But think of it this way — everyone started somewhere. You don't know what these people looked like when they first made their commitment to regular exercise, but look where they are now. Also, the folks you'll encounter at the gym are generally focused on getting a great workout, not what the others around them look like. Take this step for you!

Do not let fear hold you back from making the change you are seeking. Whether it's getting physically or financially healthy, or any other vision you have for your life, come up with an actionable, attainable 30-day goal. Visualize your intensions and write out your game plan. Certainly you can do this for just one month. At the end of the month, reassess the situation and determine what's working and what isn't. Then you can adjust and determine how you'd like to proceed from there.

# 15. Diet vs. Lifestyle Modification

*"Four . . . I don't think I could eat eight."*
**— Yogi Berra, when asked by a waitress
how many slices he wanted his pizza cut into**

What's the difference between a "diet" and lifestyle modification? In my opinion, the term *diet* is a setup for disappointment. The very nature of the word means the experience will be short-lived, because you are either on a diet or off one. And the yo-yo weight changes that result from on-again/off-again diet patterns are extremely unhealthy. For long-term success, you must have long-term commitment. Hence the term, **lifestyle modification**. Unfortunately, it's true that there are no quick fixes. We didn't gain all our weight in a week, so we can't expect to shed those unwanted pounds more quickly than we added them.

Similarly, there is no truth to the concept of "spot training." If you're doing hundreds of sit-ups with a goal of getting rid of abdominal fat, you will simply be building muscle below the fat. Overall weight loss and fat burning must occur to trim the belly. Additionally, it's very difficult to lose weight during times of stress, especially around the abdomen, because chronically elevated stress hormones contribute to fat accumulation. Therefore, it's important to work on eliminating the source of the stress.

Let's say your goal is to lose 30 pounds. What has kept you from losing the weight in the past? It is important that you identify the reason(s) so you do not continue to repeat your history. I clearly remember a particular patient who came to see me about weight loss. As I asked her questions to get a feel for her barriers to success, she shared the fact that she had been sexually abused as a child. Gaining weight was her way of appearing less attractive so that she would draw less attention to herself. I would have done her a disservice by designing an individualized weight-loss plan and sending her on her way. Getting her the psychological help she needed to deal with her traumatic past was far more crucial than anything else we could have discussed that day.

## Eating Habits vs. Exercise

Should you focus more on eating habits or increasing exercise? Obviously, both are important to your overall health. But think about this: It's about 3,500 calories that equal a pound. Over the course of a week, it's much easier to avoid taking in an extra 3,500 calories than it is to burn the same amount!

Remember, too, the combination of diet and exercise that is right for one person may not be the best for someone else. Weight loss would be easy if there was one simple formula we could all follow, but there isn't. Some people do fine with skipping breakfast, but most of us need that metabolic jump-start at the beginning of the day to lose weight. Breakfast keeps our body out of "starvation" or "hibernation" mode, holding on to fat because it doesn't know when its next meal will be.

Our calorie intake seems to expand exponentially without careful attention. Let's say you drink two 12-ounce sodas per day. One can of regular (non-diet) soda contains about 140 calories. So if you drink two per day, that's 280 calories, which adds up to 1,960 calories in a week, and 7,840 in four weeks. Wow, that's two pounds in just one month! And unless you're doing enough exercise to burn them off, those pounds are going straight onto your body.

## Making Healthy Food Choices in Restaurants

Trying to make healthy choices at restaurants can be challenging, as well. On the way home from a vacation, my friend and I had a few hours at the airport between flights. We wanted something light to eat, since we had been doing a lot of fork-to-mouth exercise on our trip. We decided on a salad at Chili's restaurant. I chose a salad called "Quesadilla Explosion." It was delicious! I even asked the waiter for the salad dressing ingredients because it was so good. Afterwards, my stomach was a little upset, but I didn't think much of it at the time.

The next time I was in the mood for a salad, my thoughts quickly returned to the Chili's salad. Again, my stomach was mildly upset after eating it. Finally I went to Chili's website to view the nutritional contents of the salad. I was shocked. The salad alone contains a whopping 980 calories, and 48 grams of fat. The delicious dressing, a citrus balsamic vinaigrette, has 340 calories, and 33 grams of fat in just two ounces. (Of course, I asked for extra dressing to top it off.) No wonder my stomach was upset!

Most restaurants, as you know, serve huge portions. Here's a trick, though. Cut the portion you will eat at the restaurant by half or so, reserving the rest to take home for a future meal(s). Avoid fried food and creamy sauces. Many restaurants now offer nutritional information about their food if you ask for it. Use this information to help you make healthy decisions.

### Watching Your Caloric Intake

Do you dislike the heavy feeling of being too full after eating a huge meal? Does post-prandial lethargy (a fancy term for feeling tired after a big meal) affect you? Eating a large meal, especially an unhealthy one with lots of simple sugars, raises the body's blood sugar level. As a result, the blood sugar drops, creating that lethargic feeling. There is no reason to feel this way. Eating healthier, small, frequent meals throughout the day can help keep your energy level up. It can help you avoid the hungry feeling which often leads to eating large meals.

It's important to keep a close eye on your total caloric intake when starting a "small but frequent" plan like this to make sure you are not taking in extra calories throughout the day.

Get rid of all of temptations in your house. Switch to whole-grain bread and light mayonnaise, or consider eating just one piece of bread instead of two. Surround yourself with only healthy food. Avoid the extra calories in alcohol. Get in the habit of reading food labels so you will know what you are consuming.

- Protein: 1 gram contains 4 calories

- Carbohydrates: 1 gram contains 4 calories

- Fat: 1 gram contains 9 calories

- Alcohol: 1 gram contains 7 calories

Learn which fats are healthy and which or not. Monounsaturated, polyunsaturated, and omega-3 fatty acids are healthier fats and can be found in nuts, avocados, and certain types of fish, such as salmon and mackerel. Unhealthy fats include saturated and trans-fats, which can be found in dairy products, red meat, crackers, cookies, and cakes.

**Keeping a Food Record**

If you are serious about weight loss, keep a detailed food record for a week, while continuing to eat normally. This will allow you to see how many and what kinds of calories you are consuming. List the food, amount eaten, and caloric intake. Note the portion sizes on food labels, as they tend to be much smaller than you might expect. For example, have you ever noticed the portion size indicated on the nutritional label of a carton of ice cream? Next time you fill your ice cream bowl, note whether you really serve yourself a half cup, as the food label describes one serving size. My bowl is probably closer to two cups! If you are eating two portion sizes, that means double the calories in your food record.

Add your totals to see how many calories you take in on a given day. Add all the totals together and divide by seven to get an average for the week. Helpful tools are available to assist you in keeping track of your intake, such as the one at www.mypyramidtracker.gov.

If your weight is reasonably stable and your total caloric intake averages about 2,000 calories a day, cutting back to 1,500 per day equals one pound of weight loss per week (500 calories multiplied by the seven days of the week equals 3,500 calories). One to two pounds a week is the ideal goal — this is the type of weight loss that will last.

# 16. Exercise-O-Rama

*If I'd known I was going to live so long,*
*I'd have taken better care of myself.*
**— Leon Eldred**

What if you were offered a pill that would help you lose weight, tone your body, reduce stress and depression, lower blood pressure, improve your quality of sleep, and help prevent heart attack, stroke, and cancer? Would you take it? Does it sound like a wonder drug? What if you could accomplish all of them without taking a pill at all? You can: all these benefits — and more — come from exercise!

Exercise is critical not only for weight control, but for overall health. Does the thought of running on a treadmill or using the elliptical  trainer at the gym appeal to you? If not, that's okay! How about taking an evening walk with a friend or your spouse? Or trying a yoga class? Taking a dance lesson? Joining a volleyball team? It's unlikely that you will stick with something you don't enjoy, so it is absolutely crucial to find something you love to do. In addition to the cardiovascular and muscular benefits of exercise, it's a great way to release stress hormones.

No time? Even a 10-minute walk during lunch is better than nothing. Schedule exercise into your Day-Timer®, just like you would any other event. Determine the time of day that works best with your body rhythm, and schedule it. If you are a morning person, get out there early. If you enjoy watching television, commercials are a great time for strength training. You don't need fancy equipment from a gym. Use your own body weight for exercises such as push-ups, and strengthen your core with sit-ups. It's helpful to seek out a trainer who can give you exercise ideas that will work for your body type and goals, as well as give you guidelines for creating a home program.

While both cardiovascular exercise and strength training are important, not all types of exercise are the best for all people. It really depends a lot on your goal. I once had a patient who was trying to lose weight through daily exercise. She has a mesomorph body type, meaning she gains muscle very easily. Her favorite exercise at the gym was the stair-stepper, because it burns calories quickly, especially when used at a high intensity. But instead of losing inches, she gained them because she continued building muscle, due to her body type. I suggested she switch to less weight-bearing activities, such as the elliptical trainer and yoga/Pilates classes. These activities, combined with healthier eating, worked much better for her.

A fantastic way to increase your awareness about your movement throughout the day is to wear a pedometer on your hip or shoe. You have probably heard suggestions about easy ways to get in shape, such as parking farther away or taking the stairs instead of the elevator. These are wonderful suggestions, yet easy to forget or disregard. But the pedometer holds you accountable as it counts your every step! A great target goal is 10,000 steps a day, which equals about five miles.

Since everyone's "normal" is different, it's helpful to wear a pedometer for a few days just to see what normal is for you. While 10,000 steps a day is a good general target goal, you may already naturally take that many or more steps per day . . . so 15,000 might be a better target for you. On the flip side, say your normal is just 3,000 steps per day. Set a smaller target first, such as 5,000 steps per day, and work up to 10,000.

Many pedometers allow you to set your stride length so that you can get a more accurate reading of how far you have walked per day.

Also, most units have a setting that enables you to increase or decrease the sensitivity of your movements. You will definitely want to play with the settings to make sure your pedometer is counting your steps as accurately as possible.

# 17. "Butt" Out

*You can set yourself up to be sick, or you can choose to stay well.*
— **Wayne Dyer**

I f you are ready to kick the smoking habit, congratulations! There are several steps you can take that will help the process tremendously. (If you are not a smoker, you can apply the following concepts to any habit you are trying to break.) First of all, identify the barriers that have kept you from quitting in the past. When you have thought about quitting, or tried to quit, what were the triggers that led you back to the cigarettes? What's your action plan for dismantling those barriers and preventing the smoking triggers from tripping you up this time?

One of my patients taught me a great trick for handling cravings. Before her quit date, she wrote down all the reasons she wanted to quit smoking. After quitting, she carried this piece of paper with her at all times. Every time she had a craving, she read her list of reasons not to light up. She continued this process for about six months, until the cravings stopped. Now, she keeps the list as a "trophy" to remind her of her success!

## Other Techniques That Can Help Ensure Your Success

- Pick a quit date and tell yourself, from the core of your being, that this date is the first day of your smoke-free life. Most of my patients like to quit smoking on a Monday so they can smoke for that one last weekend.

- As you prepare for your quit date, clean your house and car to eliminate the smell of smoke.

- Throw out the ashtrays and anything that reminds you of smoking.

- Every time you light up before the big day, think about your ultimate goal.

- Make a countdown of your cigarettes — "20, 19, 18, etc. to go, and then I'll be smoke free forever."

- Tell your supportive family, friends, colleagues, and others who will cheer you on.

- Avoid smoky places or anything associated with smoking for as long as you need to at first.

- Avoid alcohol, as it can lower your inhibitions and make it easier to pick up a cigarette.

Your healthcare provider can explain and prescribe medication to help you through the quitting process. While it's true that no drug is perfect and each has potential side-effects, several good medications are available to decrease your craving for cigarettes. This type of medication is generally started one to two weeks before the designated quit date and continued for several months.

On the actual quit date and beyond, nicotine replacement might be suggested by your healthcare provider to help with the nicotine withdrawal symptoms. It's important that you do NOT smoke while on a nicotine replacement, as this can increase your risk of cardiac events such as heart attack and stroke.

# 18. Sleep Hygiene

*Sleep is when all the unsorted stuff comes flying out,
as from a dustbin upset in a high wind.*

**— William Golding**

Having trouble sleeping at night? Maybe it's getting to sleep . . . or maybe it's staying asleep? Why? Is it the stress again? If yes, what can you do to work through it? In addition to getting to the root of your stress, the following sleep hygiene tips can help tremendously.

- Caffeine has a long half-life. That cup you drink in the  morning can potentially affect your sleep at night. Switch to decaf and avoid other caffeinated drinks throughout the day (such as some teas and soft drinks), but do this gradually, to avoid caffeine withdrawal headaches.

- Smoking is a stimulant — perhaps you can view this as added incentive to quit.

- Avoid activities such as doing paperwork or watching television in your bedroom. Your bedroom should be associated only with intimacy and sleep.

- Get into a nightly habit of preparing your body for sleep. For example, you might wash your face, brush your teeth, and read a little before going to bed each night. By following this routine, your body will begin to automatically know that rest time is approaching.

- Try to keep your body on a schedule, going to sleep and waking up at the same time on weekends as you do during the week.

- Avoid napping.

Not a morning person? Me either. Here's a trick that can help. Let's say your alarm clock is set for 6:30 a.m. Before you go to bed the night before, tell yourself you will wake up at 6:25 a.m. feeling alert, refreshed, and ready to start your day. Really imagine this as you say it — visualize the alarm clock, and your feeling upon waking, until you believe it. With proper mental preparation, you can prepare your body to utilize its own internal alarm. What a beautiful thing it is to wake up naturally when your body is ready to do so.

# 19. Lab Values

*An individual without information can't take responsibility.*
*An individual with information can't help but take responsibility.*
— **Jan Carlzon**

D oes your healthcare provider casually throw out the names of lab tests during your office visits? It's understandable if all those medical terms make you uncomfortable, as they can be quite confusing. Here are explanations for a few of the more common ones. (Note: This list is NOT meant to be all-inclusive or to replace a more comprehensive explanation by your healthcare provider.)

- Complete blood count (CBC): Indicates the red and white blood cell levels. This can help determine whether you are anemic or might have an infection.

- Basic metabolic panel (BMP) or electrolyte panel: Provides information about your kidney function, blood sugar level, and electrolytes, such as sodium and potassium. Sometimes a complete metabolic panel (CMP) is ordered, which is similar to the BMP but more comprehensive, and includes liver function tests.

- Liver function tests (LFT): As the name suggests, this is a test of the functionality of your liver. It may be used as a baseline before you start on medications that are metabolized through the liver (such as certain cholesterol-lowering medications and oral anti-fungal agents). It can also show an indication of liver damage, which can stem from excessive alcohol use, hepatitis, and other toxic causes.

- Thyroid stimulating hormone (TSH): A good screening test for thyroid function; it can help detect either hypo- or hyper-thyroid disease.

- Sedimentation rate ("Sed" rate) and C-reactive protein (CRP): Both are nonspecific tests looking for inflammation. They are not designed to diagnose any specific disease, but to help add clues to the big picture.

- Cholesterol: The total number is not as meaningful as the breakdown of the "good" (high density lipoprotein — HDL) and "bad" (low density lipoprotein — LDL) cholesterol. Here's an easy way to remember which one is which: "H" is for healthy, "L" is for lethal. So, you want your HDL to be high and your LDL to be low in order to avoid fatty build up in the arteries.

# 20. Prepare for Your Doctor Appointments

*Getting sick has at least as much to do with
how you come to the germ emotionally
as it does with how the germ physically comes to you.*
**— Carl A. Hammerschlag**

I use the term "doctor" loosely here, and include all healthcare providers, such as medical doctors, doctors of osteopathy, physician assistants, nurse practitioners, and others. Find a healthcare provider you trust and with whom you feel comfortable. If you are seeing someone new, make sure your previous provider's records are sent to your new provider prior to your appointment.

Arrive at your appointment prepared. If you have a number of questions, write them down beforehand and bring them with you.

It's frustrating to leave an appointment and later remember a question you forgot to ask. Do some research before your appointment so you will have a better understanding of what is happening with your body. With this kind of preparation, the treatment options your provider recommends will likely make more sense.

One important caveat to doing this research is that you ***not*** try to diagnose yourself. Although each symptom could indicate myriad possibilities, people sometimes jump to conclusions and fear the worst. The idea is similar to healthcare providers being advised not to treat themselves, family, or friends. It's hard to be objective when the subject is too close to home.

Also, if you do not know the name of the medications or dosages you are taking, bring them to your appointment. This will save time, reduce confusion, and decrease the potential for harmful drug interactions.

Today's society seems to have developed a tendency to want to "get something" from their doctor appointments, almost as though we feel the need to have something concrete to show for having paid for the visit and waiting to be seen by the provider. For example, let's say you have an infection you believe should be treated with antibiotics. However, when you visit your healthcare provider, he or she thinks you have a viral infection that does not require antibiotic treatment. Do you feel like you've received your "money's worth" if you do not get a prescription for an antibiotic?

In this scenario, the healthcare provider is practicing good medicine by not prescribing antibiotics. Viruses, such as the common cold or the flu, do not respond to antibiotics. Using antibiotics inappropriately actually contributes to something known as antibiotic resistance, meaning that bacteria can become stronger and less responsive, overall, to antibiotic treatment. In other words, if all you need is a fly swatter to take care of a problem, you really don't need to pull out the sledgehammer. Especially if the consequence is that, later on, the sledgehammer might not work when you really need it.

In addition to heeding the advice of your healthcare provider, it is essential that you take responsibility for your own health. Let's take another example. Say that you see your primary care provider for something psychological, like stress or anxiety. The provider gives you a pill, and you hope for the best. "Band-Aid®" fixes are fine in the short term, but it's essential that you get to the root of the problem before it becomes a chronic situation. What is causing you to feel this way? What can you do about it? And, most importantly, how can you prevent it from happening again?

# 21. Chines Medicine and the Emotions

Chinese medicine relates basic emotions to specific organs of the body. Why is this important? Well, it could be an important wakeup call. When you are sick, your body is trying to tell you something. If you get a cold or the flu, your body might be saying, "Hey, slow down! Take a break, why don't you? I need a rest." If your eyes are giving you trouble, maybe there is something in life that you don't want to "see." If your legs or knees hurt, perhaps fear is keeping you from stepping forward in life.

As complex, intelligent mechanisms, it's hard to believe our bodies would randomly choose the areas where our pain or illness arises. So when our bodies speak, we need to listen!

Let's return to our examination of Chinese philosophy, starting with the lungs. The lungs are associated with grief and sadness. This correlation makes me think of the late actor, Christopher Reeve, whom we fondly remember as Superman, and his wife, Dana. In 1995, Christopher was paralyzed after a horseback riding accident. Dana stood steadfastly by her husband,

stating, "I still love you, no matter what. You are still you." It was so inspiring to know that even after such a tragedy, he and Dana continued to change the world through their contributions to research for the disabled.

*What I do is based on powers we all have inside us; the ability to endure; the ability to love, to carry on, to make the best of what we have — and you don't have to be a 'Superman' to do it.*
— **Christopher Reeve**

Less than two years after Christopher passed away in 2004, Dana Reeve died from lung cancer. She did not smoke, the classic cause of this disease. So, was it simply coincidence that she experienced lung trouble? Or was her lung disease related to the sadness and grief over her loss? We can never know the answer to that question, but it's worth considering, since the mind and body are so intertwined.

The emotions, in Chinese medicine, include anger, joy, worry, grief, sorrow, fear, and fright, as described below. Please note that various sources have slightly different descriptions.

**Sorrow (sadness) and grief** — Associated with the lungs. Sadness and grief may be associated with lung problems, weakening of the immune system, depression, fatigue, shortness of breath, asthma, or allergies.

**Pensiveness (worry)** — Associated with the spleen and stomach. Worrying may be associated with digestive problems, a loss of appetite, or fatigue.

**Fear and fright** — Associated with the kidneys. Intense fear (described as chronic) or fright (described as acute) may be associated with kidneys problems, the lower back, joint pain, breathlessness, or palpitations.

**Anger** — Associated with the liver. Anger may be associated with liver problems, dizziness, hypertension, mental confusion, or headaches.

**Joy** — Associated with the heart. Eustress (good stress) or lack of joy may be associated with heart trouble, hysteria, difficulty concentrating, or sleeplessness.

# 22. To Panic or Not to Panic? That Is the Question

*It's not what happens to you,*
*but how you react to it that matters.*

**— Epictetus**

W hen I was a new healthcare provider just several days into the job, the secretary for the floor of the hospital where I worked received a phone call from the lab. Normally, the lab faxes over results. But when a lab value is significantly outside the normal range, indicating that a patient might be in danger, the lab calls the healthcare provider.

"We have a panic value," the secretary told me immediately.

Not knowing what to do, I ran over to an experienced physician and told her excitedly, "We have a panic value!"

She replied, "Okay, the first thing you need to do is DON'T PANIC!"

I learned a lot that day, and it wasn't just about medicine. It's not helpful to get worked up about any situation to the point where you have a difficult time doing anything about it. A much better idea is to stay calm and focus on rectifying the problem. Granted, it is human nature to panic in stressful situations, but we can train ourselves to recognize a stressful situation in the making and respond in a calm manner.

When you feel panicked, stressed, or short on time, try taking three deep breaths, followed by ten normal breaths. Count as you go, and remain focused on your inhalation and exhalation to help clear your mind before moving forward.

# 23. Introvert vs. Extrovert

*Is your energy good and your mind clear? Everybody is different,
so I don't really think there are general rules here.*
— **Andrew Weil**

I f you've ever heard of or taken the Myers-Briggs personality
assessment, you may recall that the first of four categories it
summarizes is "Introvert versus Extrovert." Contrary to what
these two terms might initially appear to describe, they are not

pointing to one type of
individual who likes to be
around people and another
who does not. Rather, these
are indicators about where
specific individuals get their
energy.

Let's say you go someplace
with hundreds or thousands
of other people, maybe
Disneyland or a large work-
related function. Do you walk
out of such an experience a
few hours later feeling
recharged and energized, or
do you feel drained and
depleted? On Friday night
after a long workweek, do you
look forward to a quiet night at home reading a book or watching a
movie? Or would you prefer a night out on the town?

- Introverts recharge through quiet time. They are energized
  by the opportunity to be alone with their thoughts and
  ideas. Only then can they go out and socialize successfully.
  Introverts tend to work best alone, and they usually have a
  few very close friends. Being around crowds can be a
  draining experience for them, leading to the need for alone
  time.

- Extroverts, on the other hand, have their batteries recharged by getting out and about. Unlike introverts, socializing and being part of the crowd gives them more energy. Extroverts tend to have many casual friends and acquaintances, in addition to those very close to them. They generally work well in groups and love to surround themselves with other people.

Chances are that you not 100 percent an introvert or 100 percent an extrovert. For example, a given situation may determine your energy level. But in general, the introvert/extrovert distinction is an insightful tool because it can help you figure out why you might be feeling drained, versus full of energy and enthusiasm.

# 24. What Is Your Learning Style?

*Teach me my most difficult concepts in my preferred style.*
*Let me explore my easiest concepts in a different style.*
*Just don't teach me all the time in your preferred style*
*and think I'm not capable of learning.*
— **Virleen M. Carlson**

Whether or not you are currently involved in a formal educational setting, we are all students from time to time. Sometimes we are students by choice, learning how to do something new, such as operating a piece of electronic equipment. But how do you learn?

When you are trying to figure out your new digital camera, are you likely to read the instruction manual, cover to cover? Play with the buttons until you get it to work? Speak to the salesperson in the store? Call the company help desk?

In this situation, you would choose your learning preference naturally. All of these are great options, but your method of taking in and processing the information may be different from someone else's.

How do you learn in other settings? Let's say you need to learn a new skill for your job, so you attend a workshop or seminar. If you are a visual person and the instructor lectures the whole time, you may find it difficult to get the picture. Therefore, it's helpful to know your learning style so you can apply your preferences and maximize the experience.

# VARK

VARK stands for visual, auditory, read/write and kinesthetic, which are the four main ways humans give and receive information. The four VARK categories, described by Fleming and Mill in 1992, are detailed below, with suggestions for each learning style. You can learn more and complete a short questionnaire to determine your learning preference at www.vark-learn.com.

- *Visual:* This learning preference indicates a better understanding from charts, graphs, arrows, and other visuals. Rewriting notes in a more visual format after a lecture can be helpful for this type of learner, as well as using highlighters, different colors, underlining, and illustrating concepts.

- *Auditory:* This learning preference indicates a better understanding from the spoken word, such as hearing a lecture. These individuals reinforce learning by discussing the topics with the instructor or classmates, and explaining the concepts in their own words into a tape recorder so they can review it later.

- *Read/Write:* This learning preference indicates a better understanding of information via the written word. Individuals who learn best in this method may have a slight advantage in the Western educational system, which tends to revolve around reading and writing assignments. One tip is to write out the information in your own words, and then go back later to read your notes.

- *Kinesthetic:* This learning preference involves a more hands-on approach, involving activities such as laboratory learning, field trips, and practical applications. This type of learner grasps the material well by understanding and recalling examples that explain the material, and by physically doing activities that reinforce the information.

- *Multimodal:* Many people fall in the "multimodal" learning preference category, meaning that information can be acquired in several ways. At first glance, this may seem like the "best" category to fall in, because regardless of how the material is presented, the learner can be flexible in receiving the information. However, multimodal learners generally need to use more than one strategy for learning. They might not fully comprehend the material by using just one modality. They may need to hear it, see it, and talk about it to fully appreciate the information.

Using the VARK method to understand how you prefer to learn and how those around you prefer to receive information can be very helpful, even in the work or home setting. You can use it as a tool for relating to others, providing information to them in a way they can comprehend and asking for information in a way *you* can understand.

When you cannot control how material is presented, you can use your preferred learning method to clarify the information. For example, if an instructor is lecturing, you can open the book or examine a handout to see if there is a visual that further explains the information. Or after the talk, you can write the information out in your own words or discuss the material with your colleagues. One caveat to note is that determining your learning style is simply a helpful first step. Knowledge is potential. Stepping into action is the heart of the matter.

# 25. Explore Your Resources

*The healthy, the strong individual, is the one*
*who asks for help when he needs it. Whether he has*
*an abscess on his knee or in his soul.*

**— Rona Barrett**

When things get too overwhelming, it's totally okay to ask for help. It's amazing how willing most people are to lend a hand, when asked. And just think about all your potential sources of assistance.

For example, I was in graduate school working on the biggest project of my education, a doctoral dissertation. For more than a year, I researched everything related to my topic and put together ideas about how to test my theory. The problem was, I didn't understand statistics. Unfortunately, this was an essential element of the project. I had barely made it through my statistics classes, getting help constantly just to complete the assignments. My brain just wasn't wired that way.

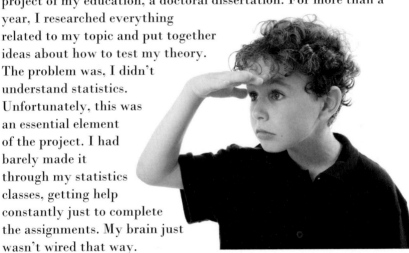

At the time, I was working for a medical research company that had a biostatistics department. I didn't have any close contacts in that area, but I called the department director, since I had met him in passing. I asked if I could stop by with a question. After presenting my idea, he explained how to design the project from a statistical standpoint. Of course! I should have known to use a linear regression analysis!

By the end of the dissertation, I made friends with everyone in the biostatistics department. They were all rooting for me, and so willing to help me, my whole way through. While it wasn't easy to ask for help from people I barely knew, I found them happy to pitch in. Often people are glad to help, even when you least expect it. But often, they don't know you need help until you ask.

Another great example of asking for and receiving help involved my process of writing this book. I pondered the question of who would be the most appropriate person to write the forward. I wanted a leader who truly embraced the body-mind-spirit philosophy. My thoughts turned to Dr. James McGovern, the former president of A.T. Still University. Andrew Taylor (A.T.) Still was the father of osteopathic medicine, founding the first osteopathic school in 1892.

I am on the faculty of this University and had met Dr. McGovern several times. I have been most impressed by the way he has truly embraced A.T. Still's vision. In each conversation I have personally had with him, and when I've heard him speaking with students, he has encouraged the "whole person" medical approach. I very much agree! Often, in today's healthcare model, medical providers as well as the patients themselves prefer to mask the symptoms instead of getting to the root of the problem. But it's only in getting to the core issue at hand that we can make great strides toward true healing.

I nervously e-mailed Dr. McGovern, requesting a meeting with him. He quickly invited me to come upstairs to his office. When I told him about this book, he was almost more excited than I was! He said he would be honored to write the forward for me. Additionally, he offered to me help me with the editing and publishing process. While I was scared to ask for help, he was more than willing to offer all his available resources.

# 26. Proceed With Confidence

*Keep your face to the sunshine and you cannot see the shadow.*
— **Helen Keller**

Imagine that you are interviewing two people for a job. The first person comes in with poor posture, infrequent eye contact, and a pretty obvious low self-image. Their weak handshake feels like a cold fish. You ask, "How are you?" and the candidate looks down and mumbles "I'm fine, thanks." Regardless of how qualified or brilliant this person is, a weak first impression can ruin an interview.

On the flip side, your next candidate walks in confidently with excellent posture, looking you right in the eye. After a firm handshake, you ask, "How are you?" This person clearly responds,

"I'm wonderful, thank you. How are you?" These first few seconds set the tone for a solid interview.

Posture is very important for both your body and image. However, it's something many of us rarely think twice about. Unfortunately, poor posture can lead to health problems, such as back or muscular pain. If you hunch over a computer all day instead of sitting up tall, you are not doing your body any favors. Try these tips for improved posture and ergonomics while sitting:

- Rest your palms (not wrists) on a support while typing.

- Your hands should be even or slightly lower than the elbows (having a keyboard mounted under your desktop can help).

- Your wrists should be straight (not cocked up or bent downwards) to prevent carpel tunnel syndrome.

- Sit up tall, resting on the back of the chair — do not slouch forward or round your back.

- Use a chair with good lumbar support. This can be added to your chair if it's not already built in.

- Adjust your chair height so that your feet are flat on the floor. Your hips should be just slightly higher than your knees.

- The computer should be right in front of your eyes, so that you are looking forward, not down or to either side.

- Do not carry a wallet in your back pocket, or remove it before sitting down. Sitting on a wallet will cause your pelvis to tilt unevenly, which can lead to back pain.

- Take frequent stretch breaks.

To practice excellent posture, pretend you are a skeleton in biology class, hanging from a hook. The hook pulls the back of your head up (with the chin tucked in ever so slightly) directly over your spine. Your shoulders fall back and down, and your chest is forward. The stomach is pulled in. Your hips are right over your feet, facing forward.

Try to picture figureheads or extremely successful people in your life. Chances are they have great posture. On the flip side, think of someone you know who has poor posture, or simply begin noticing the posture of those around you. If someone is slumped over, they probably do not appear confident. See if you notice a correlation between posture and self esteem.

Practice looking ahead, instead of down. Show the world that you are seeing the big picture. Notice your surroundings. If you look down, all you see is what's right in front of you. Imagine what would happen if people drove their cars this way! There would be accidents all the time because individual drivers were not looking at their surroundings. The same concept applies to *your* gaze. Confidently move forward, taking in everything you can see. Even if you don't *feel* confident, *looking* confident will eventually become natural, with practice. In turn, *looking* confident will help you *feel* confident. This can improve your attitude and your mood!

# 27. Fear Not

*"When an unconscious issue remains unconscious,
it shows up outside of us as fate.*

— **Carl Jung**

Is there something in life that you fear or don't handle well? Maybe it's heights, confronting people, or public speaking? My fear was death. This was probably related to my training as a healthcare provider. In this profession, we do everything humanly possible to keep people alive. For someone to die is a failure on my part, or so I believed. The problem was, this belief was beginning to affect my career . . . so I finally decided to do something about it.

I signed up for a hospice volunteer training class, and afterward was assigned my first patient. I only visited her a few times before she passed away. But through my relationship with this woman, I learned a lot about the human side of death. I began to view death as a natural part of life and got over my fear.

Maybe your fear involves your career. Is there a job you hesitate to apply for because you worry you are not completely qualified? Go ahead and submit your application — you have nothing to lose. Maybe you have other qualities the potential employer finds desirable, qualities that just might land you the job. You will never know if you don't try. The best possible scenario would be that you land the job; the worst thing would be that you don't get the job. That'd be okay, too, because that would simply mean it was not the best job for you, and that something better was in the works.

Or maybe it's a sabbatical or a move you want to make, but it's hard to leave everything you already know? A friend told me about her dream to visit Israel, the Holy Land. "But it is so unstable there," she explained, "and the news every day confirms that it's crazy to consider visiting." She expressed these concerns to someone older and wiser, and his response had a profound impact on her. He told her he once had friends who always wanted to go to Israel. They kept waiting and waiting for a safe time to go. They wanted to go at a time when the fighting had calmed down so that they would feel comfortable. As they continued to wait, they grew older, eventually passing away without ever making the trip. "If you want to go on this trip," he said, "go." The same is true for whatever you are putting off. There is no reason to wait. It will never be safe — but look at what you have to gain by doing it.

Take on your challenge. Climb a small hill and start facing your fear of heights. Join a Toastmasters group to develop your public speaking skills. If that still feels intimidating, you can even start by speaking in front of a mirror or to your pet. Go for it. Living in fear keeps you from moving forward in life.

Psychologist Scott Bennett expands on the "fear-full" truth:

> As a psychologist, I have one fantasy. I want to teach the world that there is absolutely nothing to fear. Nothing! Virtually every bit of our human suffering is the consequence of fear. We fear the future — but the future does not exist beyond a concept. It is not here yet. Yes, there is a place for planning, but don't let it take over your life to the point where you are always planning but never experiencing. On the other hand, we lament the past, but the past no longer exists outside of our memories. In fact, all of our suffering is rooted in things that do not exist!

> The only place we can truly live is in the present. Perhaps the most poignant example of this is when we are in the state of "flow." That is, when we are so engrossed in an activity that time ceases to exist. What seems like 20 minutes turns out to be several hours. This is what it means to be "totally in the now."

*But alas, it's more complicated than that. We all fantasize about do-overs for our mistakes, and we hope that nothing bad happens to us in the future. I am not advocating being careless or reckless with our lives, nor am I suggesting that we should not think about the future or not learn from our past. What I am advocating is a change in attitude that keeps us mindful about treating life with care and attention. Embrace the present moment and notice it. Notice life.*

*To fear means you do not trust yourself or the world. To the degree that we allow ourselves to live in fear, we perpetuate it all around us. I say, be bold, be careful, be yourself. You are just fine. In fact, you are better than fine — you are amazing.*

# 28. Is Your Career Living Up to Your Expectations?

*We are at our very best, and we are happiest, when we are
fully engaged in work we enjoy on the journey toward
the goal we've established for ourselves. It gives meaning
to our time off and comfort to our sleep. It makes everything
else in life so wonderful, so worthwhile.*

**— Earl Nightingale**

Do you remember why you went into your chosen career?
Are you satisfied with your work? Have you considered
your higher purpose? What is it that you *really* want to do?
Make an impact on people's lives? For folks who go into
the healthcare field, a common (that is, generic) response to this
question is, "I want to help people." Whatever
your answer is to this question, are you meeting that goal?

I began my career as a healthcare
provider. I wanted to make an
impact on the health of those around
me, yet I wasn't feeling like I had
fully met my goal. I saw about 20
patients a day. That adds up to
about 80 a week, more than 4,000
per year. But still, it was never
enough. I've come to believe
that anyone (with the proper
training) could treat sore
throat, urinary tract
infection, or knee pain of
the person in front
of me. I thought
about it and
realized that the
time I made the
most impact was when I was counseling. Talking with patients
about lifestyle modification such as weight control, smoking
cessation, and stress management was the highlight of my day.
Getting to the core of the problem was key. What were their barriers

to success and how could they manage or overcome those obstacles? How and why did the behavior begin in the first place? What purpose was it serving? How could growth come from the experience?

Eventually, I began teaching future healthcare providers. If there is one thing (or, hopefully, many more than one) I can say or do over the course of their studies that will make them better, more caring healthcare providers, I have done my job. This is now my way of helping *more* people. Let's say my class of 70 students eventually each see 20 patients a day. *My hope is that I have touched lives exponentially.* That's 1,400 patients a day . . . 7,000 a week . . . 364,000 a year.

But maybe this is still not enough. Perhaps I want to help more people still, and that is why you are holding this book in your hands. If I have touched your life in some way, small or huge, my goal has been achieved.

What are you doing to live up to your goals? How are you fulfilling your life's purpose?

# 29. The Dreaded Assignment

*Nothing is accidental in the universe — this is one of my Laws of Physics — except the entire universe itself, which is Pure Accident, pure divinity.*

**— Joyce Carol Oates**

Is there anything you are dreading? If so, what good can come of it? How can you turn it from a fearful experience into an amazing experience?

I remember hearing the story of a writer who works for an Arizona newspaper. As a new reporter, she was eager to write, but often got stuck with the assignments no one else wanted. One day, she was given an assignment to interview and write about a man who was dying. While chatting with him, she started putting

together the story of his life. The project began as a simple, one-time story. But there was so much positive feedback from the newspaper's readers that it turned into a series.

Each day, the newspaper ran an article revealing a bit more of the story of this man's life. He was told that he only had a short time to live, yet he kept on living so that he could read the next edition of the newspaper. The reporter became personally involved. This man was no longer just a story — she really cared about him, his life, and his family. Eventually, she wrote a book about her experience telling his story. As a published author who was touched by one man's life, she certainly made the most of an assignment that no one else wanted.

What assignments are you dreading? Have you taken any time to consider the deeper reason this project was given to you? Might there be something you are supposed to learn from the experience? How can you grow from it? What good can come out of it? How can you turn it into a positive experience?

# 30. Frustrations, Frustrations

*When one door closes, another opens. But we often look*
*so regretfully upon the closed door that we don't see*
*the one that has opened for us.*

**— Helen Keller**

We have all experienced them. Perhaps you didn't get the promotion you were hoping for. Or someone you thought you had made a connection with never called you back. Or your child needed extra attention while you were rushing to get out of the house in the morning. But maybe these things happened for a reason.

Is it possible that the job was going to be more stressful than you had anticipated? Could it be that the person who didn't call you back wasn't a quality person you needed in your life to begin with? What if the few extra minutes you gave your child in the morning

gave her new self-confidence to face the day?

Try not to dwell on the frustrations; whenever possible, dwell instead on the positive side of the situation. You just never know. If you believe that "for everything, there is a reason," think about the wording. It doesn't say, "for *most* things, there is a reason." It's *everything*.

One helpful technique to try when dealing with frustrating people is to flip the situation. Say that someone storms into your office, yelling. Does it do any good to fight back? Take control of the situation. Try saying something like this: "I'm happy to discuss this with you if you would like to talk. However, I will not attempt a yelling match with you since it will not solve the problem effectively. I'd like to share my side of the story if you are willing to listen. Would you like to take a seat?" This puts you in control of the situation. If the other person continues the childish behavior, that's their problem. But you've let them know in a kind but firm manner that you will not tolerate it.

# 31. What Are You Tolerating?

*The first step to getting the things you want out of life is this:*
*Decide what you want.*

**— Ben Stein**

**D**o you have "tolerations" in your everyday environment — things around the house you see every day and have been meaning to do something about? Don't let these tolerations drain you. Maybe it's something that needs to be fixed, or a scuff on the wall that needs to be painted over. Every time you see this, it briefly consumes your attention, yet instead of actually remedying the situation, you add it to your ever-growing pile of other things to do.

What can you do to create the energy to address these tolerations? Make a to-do list, and check them off as you go. Ask for help, if you need it. Just attending to one or two things per weekend can make a big difference in a relatively short period of time. If it's a larger project, break it up into smaller tasks so it's not as overwhelming.

What about friendship tolerations? Are there people in your life you would rather avoid, yet you're simply in the habit of being friends with them? I often hear people speak about this or that "friend," when that person is really just an energy sucker. He or she wants your time and resources, but offers little, if anything, in return. This drama has been playing out for years, and you feel obligated to help this person. After all, maybe there is no one else for your "friend" to turn to! How could this person survive without your help? You would be a terrible person to give up on this one-sided friendship, because they NEED you, right?

No! You are actually doing this person a great disservice by allowing their continued dependence on you. Instead of calling a spade a spade, it's time for you to call a parasite a parasite. Perhaps without realizing it, you have allowed a parasitic type of relationship to develop, where one entity consistently feeds off the other — the host. Have you ever considered that this person is very likely using you as a crutch, rather than seeking their own path of personal growth?

Our goal should be to create symbiotic relationships, ones in which each individual benefits. You take turns helping one another out, and leaning on each other during tough times. This is the very essence of a give-and-take relationship.

Take a look at the tolerations in your life. Imagine how much better you will feel when you stop tolerating people and situations that no longer serve you.

# 32. Conflict - A Spiritual Opportunity

*A Native American grandfather was talking
to his grandson about how he felt. The grandfather
said: "I feel as if I have two wolves fighting in my
heart. One wolf is the vengeful, angry, violent
one. The other wolf is the loving, compassionate one."*

*The grandson asked him,
"Which wolf will win the fight in your heart?"*

*The grandfather answered: "The one I feed."*
**— Native American Story**

Psychologist Scott Bennett explains:

*Not many people thrive on conflict. It elicits unpleasant
connotations of fighting, aggression, disappointment, and
anger. There's simply nothing fun about it. It is human nature
to react and become defensive when we feel attacked, wronged, or
threatened. From a biological standpoint, it may appear as if we
are always ready for*

*battle, so before we
know it, we are
emotionally
hijacked. Game on.*

*But in the context of
spiritual growth
opportunities, such
a preprogrammed
response does not
need to compete.*

*That is, if we are bold, we can control our response so that no
battle takes place. The challenge is to remain open, which
requires an attitude of mindfulness.*

*For example, if a person says something to you that is hostile or
incorrect, you have options. You could get in their face and
"give it right back to them." Another more mindful option would*

be to note your own reaction as purely defensive (which is little more than one's ego being bruised) and give yourself some room to decide how to proceed.

Regarding mindfulness, you must realize and accept that people act angrily when they are hurt, scared, confused, or otherwise feeling threatened. So the only logical or healthy response would be to remain calm and try to promote an exchange of ideas. This is integrity at work. If you allow yourself to be overly affected by the actions of another, you give away your power and lose integrity — and then blame the other person for how you are feeling and acting! Hey, who's in charge here?

Often, something transformative happens when we successfully pull this off. The attacker unconsciously dislikes his or her own behavior and may quickly become calmer while backing off from their aggressive stance. Remember, they too have felt threatened and are only behaving as they have been taught to. However, reacting in a similar fashion to their aggression only adds fuel to the fire and escalates the conflict. Why make their ugly behavior about you? Instead, figure out what the real, underlying issue is. Let them talk, vent, and express themselves. They'll feel better, but you are under no obligation to agree with them. More importantly, you are under no obligation to disagree with them, either.

People often confuse the notions of understanding and agreement. They are, at best, conceptual cousins. One must understand in order to agree, yet one doesn't necessarily have to agree to understand. Allowing the attacker his or her own thoughts, beliefs, feelings, and perceptions is a respectful position. By soliciting a greater understanding of the attacker, even your own need to be understood diminishes.

Additionally, by withholding a counterattack, you are being respectful to yourself. This does not imply that you should ever tolerate abuse or violence. Rather, it simply means that you will no longer contribute destructive forces to the Universe. This tactic worked for Gandhi and Martin Luther King, and it can work for you, too.

*However, remember that to deny another their right to think and believe as they do only promotes hostility and defiance. Such a stance is doomed to failure. Thankfully, it failed for Hitler, Stalin, and Hussein. It will fail you, also.*

*It takes tremendous courage to risk being wrong, to take the high road, and to face conflict. It requires compassion for another human being, patience with them, and a respect for their differences. It takes intellect and faith in a greater purpose. These are the good things about human nature. To fight or run from conflict changes nothing, typically makes things worse, and promotes harm and bad feelings. These are some of the worst characteristics of human nature. The difference between the two is the difference between power, which is healing and affirming — and force, which is disempowering and destructive.*

*Putting all of this into practice takes practice. We are not generally taught to be quite so compassionate toward others and ourselves. But the successes are infectious, and they help diminish an unhealthy reliance on our animal instincts. These instincts are there in case of actual life-and-death threats. But really, how much of life is truly life-threatening?*

# 33. Finding the Hidden Treasure in Tragedy

*No one is in control of your happiness but you; therefore,
you have the power to change anything about yourself
or your life that you want to change.*
— **Barbara de Angelis**

No matter how much we'd rather it didn't, tragedy happens. It's difficult, if not impossible, to avoid all traumas and tragedies as we journey through life, whether they affect us directly or indirectly. In fact, experiencing difficult times can help us better appreciate the good times.

Psychologist Scott Bennett explains how, through his years as a practicing psychologist, he has been reminded daily that nothing is for certain, and that control is an illusion we've created to provide comfort in an uncertain world. On the other hand, he is also impressed every day at people's resilience and willingness to introspect and find deeper meaning in their life experiences.

Consider these questions as they relate to a recent trauma you or someone you know might have experienced:

1. How can you make sense of the event?
2. What made you particularly susceptible to the event?
3. What does this event convey to you from the standpoint of being vulnerable?
4. How were you changed physically by what happened?
5. How were you changed mentally by what happened?
6. How were you changed emotionally by what happened?
7. How were you changed spiritually by what happened?
8. What bad results came from the event?

9. What good results came from the event?

10. How were loved ones affected by what happened?

11. How has your view of family life been impacted by what happened?

12. How might your life be different if the event had never happened?

13. Are there any ways in which you've seemed to need this event in order to grow and feel more alive?

14. What did the event take out of you?

15. What did the event add to your life?

16. What did the event add to your family's life?

17. How were your faith, beliefs, and general understanding of life affected by the event?

18. Can you imagine how your life could be positively changed as a result of the event?

19. Is there anything you learned from your experience that could be of benefit to others?

20. How are you okay despite having endured the event?

As you can see from this type of inquiry, the questions are designed to help you get out of victim mode. They help you start thinking about the event in more constructive ways, while still acknowledging the unpleasantness of the situation. This is often the transition from victim identity, through resilience and survivor modes, into a more thriving existence.

Philosopher Friedrich Nietzsche stated, "That which does not kill me makes me stronger." We cannot work around, over, under, or away from difficult events when they happen. We must face our fears and work through them if we are to overcome them.

When you find yourself contemplating the reasons an event has occurred, revisit the questions above to help facilitate your emotional growth.

# 34. Seeing the Big to Understand the Small

*When you examine the lives of the most influential people
who have ever walked among us, you discover one thread that
winds through them all. They have been aligned first with their
spiritual nature and only then with their physical selves.*
— **Albert Einstein**

Sometimes, it's tough to look at the big picture when we are focused only on one tiny aspect of a situation. I often see my students get upset when things don't go their way. Classes start too early, the test questions were confusing, the lecture was boring, or the schedule changed unexpectedly.

What may be going on behind the scenes is that the early hour was the only time a particular classroom was available or it was the only time that fit a given professor's schedule . . . or they didn't understand the test questions because they didn't study enough. Through grumblings initiated by their limited

 understanding of the circumstances, the same students may miss the fact that behind the scenes, the faculty works tirelessly to give them a great education so they can ultimately treat and care for patients. And while the students have a right to hope their classes will be interesting, a fantastic education doesn't always involve Oscar-worthy lectures.

Imagine an actress doing a scene from a play. Can she truly understand and portray the complexity of the character after studying only one scene? Probably not. In order to give the best performance, she will read the full play and ask the writer and/or director questions so she can better understand her own role and the specific scene.

Another way to imagine this concept is to think of something small, like the normal, healthy bacteria that live in your body. These little guys are so tiny that they are invisible to the naked eye. Yet when examined under a microscope, a whole alternate world emerges.

So in life, when a situation doesn't make sense or is frustrating, keep in mind that there may be much more to the picture than what you can perceive.

# 35. When in a Pickle

*It makes no sense to worry about things you have no control
over because there's nothing you can do about them,
and why worry about things you do control?
The activity of worrying keeps you immobilized.*
— **Wayne Dyer**

L et's say you are facing a situation over which you really
have very little control. Maybe it's someone you *have* to
work with, or it's going to be one more month before you
can get out of your contract with a roommate. It doesn't do
any good to focus on the negative situation; in fact, doing so just
intensifies the problem. Try to look for something positive about the
person or situation. Focus on the good qualities or aspects, however
small they might be. Such a shift in perspective may not fix the
situation, but it can at least make it more tolerable.

Life is about what you focus on, so it makes sense to focus on the
positive. To take full
responsibility for your life,
you must be aware of your
intentions in every
moment, in every situation.
Useful questions include:
"What is my intention
here?" or "What is my
goal?" Intentions work best
when you are fully present
in the situation. Ask for the
result you want, and intend
for it to happen.

Let's say you have been
feeling stressed at work
lately. So, your goal is to
have a smooth, wonderful
day at the office tomorrow.
Before falling asleep, visualize a fantastic day awaiting you. See

yourself waking up feeling refreshed, getting ready for work efficiently, driving in without traffic delays, greeting everyone with a big smile on your face, handling problems easily and comfortably, getting along well with the boss, and making a positive difference in the lives of those around you. In addition to visualizing this, feel it as well.

When you wake up the next morning, briefly repeat this process by imagining the best aspects of the day ahead. You can even imagine that something unexpected and pleasant will happen. Those around you will feel your vibrational shift. Doing this exercise and reminding yourself of it throughout the day will set the stage for a more joyful experience.

# 36. Don't Touch the Rice

*If a man does not keep pace with his companions perhaps
it is because he hears a different drummer. Let him step
to the music he hears, however measured or far away.*
— **Henry David Thoreau**

Recently I went on a sushi kick, determined to make delicious California rolls on my own. Somehow, no matter how hard I tried, they were never quite as tasty as the ones in the restaurants. I was convinced it had to do with my rice cooking technique, because my rice never turned out quite right. I tried various methods, adding more or less water, using rice vinegar and sugar, and trying to stir constantly so it would all cook evenly.

A friend came to visit, and in her honor, I set out on a mission to make an amazing sushi dinner. After explaining my rice problem, she said to me, "Don't touch the rice." I wasn't quite sure what to think about that. How could I not touch it if I was going to make it correctly? But I did as she said. Who knew it would turn out perfectly?!

Likewise, in life we sometimes get embroiled in situations we should stay out of; at those times, it's best to just leave everything alone and let the situation work itself out. This can be challenging, because we innately want to help. Sometimes, not getting involved can feel much more difficult than trying to help. But allowing others to grow and learn on their own is sometimes the best help of all.

Let the person know you are there to support them if they need you. Just saying these words, instead of offering your opinion, will allow you to simply listen and be more fully present to the situation. Give the other person the opportunity to brainstorm possible solutions to their crisis. Sometimes, it's just best "not to touch the rice."

# 37. I'll Get to It, Someday

*As long as you know what it is you desire, then by simply
affirming that it is yours – firmly and positively,
with no ifs, buts, or maybes – over and over again,
from the minute you arise in the morning until the time you
go to sleep at night, and as many times during the day as your
work or activities permit, you will be drawn to those people,
places, and events that will bring your desires to you.*
— **Scott Reed**

Do you have a secret dream or goal? Maybe it's to go back to school or learn how to dance? Maybe it pops up in the back of your mind every once in a while, and you tell yourself, "I'll do that someday, when I have the time."

The thing is, someday never gets here. Extra time never arrives. *You have to make time.* Go for it.

I used to work with a woman who always wanted to go to nursing school. "When my kids get older," she'd tell herself. As her children grew, though, they had new needs. Reasons and excuses can always get in the way, or justify, *NOT* doing something. Instead, think about the reason *TO* do whatever "it" may be for you. Start with baby steps. If your goal is a nursing degree, for example, start by taking one class each semester. Beginning the process opens the door

for long-term success, and moving toward your goal affirms how much you love and respect yourself.

One of my goals was to write a book. In my mind, the process involved writing a detailed outline for the book, figuring out the sequence of chapters, and such. This seemed like a huge, daunting task, and therefore I avoided it for a long time. But the writing idea stayed with me, and one day I just started putting my thoughts on paper. I knew one topic I wanted to include was stress and its affects on the body. So I started writing that chapter, and the rest blossomed from there.

I realized I didn't prefer to write in traditional chapters. I had so many topics to write about, all with the common theme of the body-mind-spirit connection. So I decided to abandon the format of a normal book and write from my heart. Had I tried to force myself to do it the other way, you might not be reading this book right now.

# 38. What Percent Do You Give?

*The potential of the average person is like a huge ocean unsailed,*
*a new continent unexplored, a world of possibilities waiting*
*to be released and channeled toward some great good.*
— **Brian Tracy**

A wise high school band director once made a speech during a concert in front of his students and their parents. He posed the question, "How does band prepare students for life? How is it different from their other classes? In most schools, students can pass a class with scores as low as 70 percent. *Can you imagine how a band concert would sound if the students only hit 70 percent of the notes?"*

What a profound question! What if your surgeon only got it right 70 percent of the time? What about *your* profession? What about your *life*? I have a cute little sign in my bedroom that says, "The rest of your life begins today." How true.

Making today count will only lead to a better tomorrow. But if we simply go through the motions, the day is wasted because we haven't been authentic to ourselves. Not being fully present is like allowing your shadow to show up instead of the real you. Have you reached out to someone today? Have you spoken from the heart? If not, make it a goal for tomorrow.

One trick to giving your all — being truly present — is to stop wearing your watch. Of course, you may sometimes need it in a work situation, or to make sure you are on time for an event. But too often, we are ruled by time. We look at our watch or the clock on our cell phone to see how much time we have left before moving on to the next event. That gets our mind thinking about what is to come, rather than staying focused on what is happening in the moment.

How often have you checked the time and decided you were hungry or tired? Of course it's time to eat because you've noticed it's lunchtime or dinnertime or bedtime. Just for a day, try listening to your body instead of being ruled by time.

# 39. Rid the Clutter, Physically and Mentally

*Out of clutter, find simplicity. From discord, find harmony.*
*In the middle of difficulty lies opportunity.*
— **Albert Einstein**

If your home or office is full of clutter, it may be difficult to think clearly. ***Physical clutter equals mental clutter.*** You may want to get rid of it, but feel the task is daunting. Having a hard time doing it alone? Find an accountability partner. Challenge yourself and those around you to give this a try. Start with the big stuff, the obvious piles. Then get down to the smaller spaces, one by one.

Every week, pick a new drawer, closet, area of the garage, etc. If you haven't used it in a year or more, donate it. Recognize and honor your giving nature. What you perceive as junk may be gold to someone else.

Imagine how it would feel to start your day in a totally organized, pristine office. Would you get more work done? Would you feel calmer and more centered? Would you feel less stressed? Would it be worth the few extra minutes each day to keep everything neat? Would you save yourself time and frustration in the long run?

What about coming home to a clean house? Would there be a more relaxed nature to your sanctuary? Would you feel more organized? Again, would it be worth the few minutes of daily effort?

While feng shui may be viewed as a New Age trend, it's hard to argue with some of the big concepts like clearing clutter and getting rid of items no longer in use. Doing this makes room for clear thinking and opens the door for new aspects of your life to prosper.

# 40. Manure Happens

*One of God's greatest gifts is unanswered prayers.*
**— Garth Brooks**

How often does life unfold exactly as we plan? No so often, of course. Since this is a fact of life, it makes no sense to fight this reality. If we do, we may find ourselves in a perpetual state of frustration and disappointment. In other words, to the degree to which we resist this reality, we suffer.

All of us have had the experience of feeling extremely disappointed when an event did not unfold the way we anticipated, only to later be surprised and pleased that we did not get our way. Instead of what we originally envisioned, something greater and more wonderful was waiting.

Psychologist Scott Bennett explains:

*This experience does not have to be a rare event. All that is required is an open mind and a little faith, with imagination. One must be willing to let go of the disappointment and risk embracing the yet-to-be-known. This is how we grow. Our human capacity for adaptation is at work when we do this.*

*Manure, if explored only at face value, may be unpleasant, but we feed the world from this stuff — fertilizer! This is not a Pollyanna notion of an ever-optimistic, never-pessimistic existence. Rather, it's reality, with a positive twist.*

*The only healthy option is to keep looking for the good in any situation, for it is there and it is our salvation. Experience tells us that being patient and holding strong in our beliefs is ultimately food for our psychological immune system, and this system will not falter.*

# 41. Don't Take It Personally

*Self-actualized people are independent*
*of the good opinion of others.*

**— Wayne Dyer**

In his book, *The Four Agreements*, Don Miguel Ruiz writes, "Don't take anything personally — nothing others do is because of you. What others say and do is a projection of their own reality, their own dream. When you are immune to the opinions and actions of others, you won't be the victim of needless suffering."

So why do we take things personally? It is human nature to see situations in terms of ourselves. As babies, we are totally selfish. The world exists to fulfill our needs — and when our needs are not fulfilled, we cry or scream. But as adults, we realize that everyone else has personal needs and aspirations which take priority in their relationships. When others do not meet our expectations, it is not our fault.

Once you understand this, you can begin to notice how you react to people and situations. Are you in charge of your emotions, or are they in charge of you? Don't try to change your reaction immediately. Just mentally observe it for a short time. Soon, you will be able to decide naturally whether you wish to react or not.

We cannot take full responsibility for others. Let's say you want to offer seminars to teach people how to better manage their finances. This sounds like a great idea in theory because you can potentially help a lot of people. But what if not everyone who attends your seminar is helped? What if someone doesn't get your message? Does this mean you have failed?

It would be foolish to expect all of your students to absorb everything you teach. But those who are ready and willing will get what they need. This goes back to the Buddhist proverb, "When the student is ready, the teacher will appear." We cannot take responsibility for other people's successes or failures. Our job is simply to find our purpose in life — and in our careers.

# 42. Tell Me Something Positive

*We are not physical beings having a spiritual experience;
we are spiritual beings having a physical experience."*
— **Teilhard de Chardin**

Have you ever felt your mood being brought down by a close friend or relative who is very negative? Did you notice how conversation with that person drains your energy? Being a good listener is a wonderful trait, but if you have a habit of enabling the other person to focus on the negative, it's time to redirect the conversation.

Try asking your friend to **tell you something positive**. Focusing on the positive changes everything. Get back in touch with the joyous nature of your spirit.

Refocusing in this way lightens the mood, gives you both energy, and brings your attention back to the positive aspects of life. Do not underestimate the power of this simple perspective shift!

On the flip side, how often are **you** the negative one? Do you ever get on your own nerves? Negativity, stress, and anger are energy drainers. It's like carrying around a heavy suitcase in each hand, dragging you down and zapping your energy. What would it be like to feel a zest for life again? Self-realization and discovering your passion in life — while identifying and letting go of the "suitcases" — will set you free.

# 43. A Delicious Feedback Sandwich

*Feedback is the breakfast of champions.*
— **Ken Blanchard**

H ave you ever had to give someone constructive feedback, or correct a child? A great technique is the feedback sandwich. Say something positive, then give the necessary feedback, and end on a positive note.

I once set up a healthcare lecture series for students, taught by a physician. On the first day, the doctor told a somewhat off-color joke to get their attention. Some thought it was funny, but others were offended. This was quickly brought to the attention of the boss, who sternly told the instructor that this kind of behavior would not be tolerated, and if he wished to continue working with us, he would

need to straighten up his act. The doctor was taken aback and quite upset by the situation.

Consider another way of handling the same situation, using the feedback sandwich technique. For example, what if the boss had said instead:

"Thank you for the hard work you put into this lecture. You did a great job presenting the material. One area we need to work on, though, is the joke you told at the beginning of your presentation, because some of the students found it offensive. I realize that you used it to make a point, but it wasn't all that well received. Overall though, we appreciate you so much for taking such an interest in our students and presenting your great information to them."

Doesn't that feel much different? And yet it still gets the point across.

In addition to the feedback sandwich, simply offering positive feedback in general conversation is crucial to those around you. It makes people feel good about themselves and work harder when they realize that you notice their dedicated effort. Imagine you are hard at work as usual, and your boss comes over to tell you what a good job you are doing. Wow, what a great feeling to be appreciated!

How often do you give positive feedback to those around you? Why not give it a try? Even if the person isn't quite up to speed, find something positive to mention. Maybe their desk is always neat, or they can solve computer glitches. Let them know you appreciate them and watch how it changes both of your perspectives.

# 44. Communicating "I Feel..."

*To effectively communicate, we must realize that we are all different in the way we perceive the world, and use this understanding as a guide to our communication with others.*

— **Anthony Robbins**

A fantastic tool for communication is the term, "I feel . . ." Let me explain. Let's say that your boss constantly criticizes your work, no matter how much effort you put into it. Day after day, he criticizes you, and you've had enough! You finally work up the courage to say something. One method would be to say, "You're always on my case. Nothing I do is ever good enough. Blah-blah-blah." The problem with this approach is that, while you are standing up for yourself, this usually is interpreted as an attack, serving only to immediately put the boss on the defensive.

A more effective way to communicate would be to say, "I feel that my work is not meeting your approval. It is difficult for me to work, day after day, feeling that I am not doing my job effectively. Is there anything that I *am* doing well? What can I do to improve?"

This response, while conveying essentially the same message, opens the door for communication because it keeps the playing field — offensive versus defensive — even.

The same technique works well in personal relationships. Instead of accusing the other person of doing — *insert your pet peeve here* —, tell them how you feel when this occurs. For example, let's say your spouse is working many more hours than usual. One method would be to say, "Why are you spending so much time at work? Is work more important than your family? Where are your priorities? What are you doing there all the time?"

Or, you could start the conversation by saying, "I feel hurt that you are spending so much time at the office because it's taking away from our family time. I miss you. How can we find a better balance?"

I remember a situation when my boss believed I had used a corporate credit card for a personal expense. Instead of asking me about the purchase, she accused me, stating that my actions could lead to dismissal from the corporation. The reality was that the purchase was for a perfectly legitimate business purpose. My boss had simply forgotten the details of a previous conversation in which she had authorized the purchase. Instead of getting defensive, I simply said to her, "I feel hurt because you assumed I was doing something inappropriate, rather than asking me about the situation."

So when a situation arises that doesn't seem or feel right, ask about it, instead of making assumptions or accusations. And when approaching another person about a concern or problem, state how you feel instead of launching what will likely be perceived as an attack. A little communication can save a lot of hurt feelings.

# 45. Just Tell Us Why

*You people are telling me what you think I want to know.*
*I want to know what is actually happening.*
— **Creighton Abrams**

It is human nature to resist change because the unknown is scary. One day a student taught me a lesson in change and its relationship to communication.

My students' class schedule occasionally changes, and I am responsible for communicating this information to them. As soon as I know the details, I send the students an e-mail letting them know of the change in plans. No matter how often I used to do this, it always seemed to be met with resistance and frustration. "What is their problem?" I would find myself wondering. "They don't know what's going on behind the scenes. If I could have kept things as they were, I obviously would have done so."

One day, this topic came up during a casual conversation with a student, and she shared some wise words with me. "We're okay with change and know that things come up from time to time, but let us know why. Tell us what's going on to cause the change, so we can understand." From that point on, I have done so, and it has made a big difference in their reaction to change!

On a similar note, I often send students e-mails, asking them to stop by my office. When I simply asked them to come by without offering any explanation, they often assumed the worse. Maybe they had failed a class, or something terrible had happened. So I began stating the reason for my request in my e-mails, even if it wasn't good news. Stating my basic reason for requesting the office visit relieved their stress.

Clear communication goes a long way in forming relationships built on trust. Don't assume that you are boring someone with details when these details can actually clarify a situation. Providing explanations leads to better buy-in by those who are affected. This leads to decreased frustration and improved functioning as a team.

# 46. Connections to the Universe and Its People

> *There are no extra pieces in the universe. Everyone is here because he or she has a place to fill, and every piece must fit itself into the big jigsaw puzzle.*
> — **Deepak Chopra**

Simply put, when we do what is good for the Universe, the Universe responds in kind. The Universe does not judge us, condemn us, or punish us. The Universe is not in the business of emotional blackmail. Nor does the Universe reward us for specific acts. It is important to recognize that every **thing**, every **person**, every **thought**, and every **intention** are all parts of this unfathomable Universe.

Psychologist Scott Bennett explains:

*There are an infinite number of ways to do good things for the Universe. For example, when we are kind to ourselves by caring for our physical and mental health, the Universe responds in kind with a functional body and mind. When we are kind to others by caring for their well-being, the Universe responds with a strong sense of belonging through solid friendships and communities. And when we are kind to the planet by being good stewards of the environment, we are provided with clean air and water, and an abundance of fascinating places to explore.*

*When we carelessly pollute the environment and use its resources only for fun and profit, the Universe responds with high rates of cancer and natural disasters. When we actively and consciously hold healthy thoughts and intentions, the Universe responds with opportunities to further our good intentions. But here's the rub. When we look for something specific as a reward, we prohibit the process from manifesting anything good for us. That is, if our intention is ultimately self-serving, we are being selfish with the Universe, and it responds to that.*

*Let's take an extreme example. If I drink too much and lose my ability to control my thoughts and actions, I become drunk. I am not treating my body with respect, and I risk harming others, due to my impaired judgment. The Universe may respond with a ticket from a police officer or an injury. Or a business deal might fall through the next day because I've missed an early morning appointment.*

*If we assume we know exactly how the Universe is going to respond, we are kidding ourselves and attempting to play God. When we take such an arrogant stance, the Universe will respond unfavorably.*

*The message is simple: Do good deeds and have integrity in your actions simply for the sake of doing so. Think well simply for the sake of having good thoughts. Take care of yourself and others, and take care of the environment, simply for the sake of preserving our home and ability to live happily within it. We get what we give in all things and in all ways.*

Years ago, I learned some basic sign language. Because I used it infrequently, I forgot most of it and was embarrassed to try to communicate via sign language after all that time. Then I met a deaf woman and we became friends. When I realized just how small the deaf community was, it became clear that what I perceived as my clumsy attempt at communication was incredibly meaningful to her. She was delighted and grateful that I attempted to use her language. It didn't matter that I had forgotten many of the signs, or mixed them up. She understood what I was trying to say. Just the fact that I attempted communication meant the world to her.

Reach out to the people around you, even though it can be tough to feel a connection with someone who is very different. Maybe this person is from another country, is of a different religion or belief system, or has a disability. Recognize your hesitation and try to connect anyway. You may be amazed at the response you receive.

# 47. Relationships 101

*Two halves have little choice but to join;*
*And yes, they do make a whole*
*but two wholes when they coincide . . .*
*That is beauty,*
*That is love.*

**— Peter McWilliams**

Life coach, Alden Witte, offers the following on relationships:

## Finding the Good Prospects

Odds are, there is virtually no difference between the people you currently associate with and the choice of your next intimate partner. How much do you trust, respect, and enjoy the company of the people with whom you spend your time? While this seems like a simple question, its implications are quite profound. Answering this may very well give you insight into the type of person you might choose. Don't expect your next partner to be mature, financially stable, and loving . . . if most of the people you spend time with attract drama into their lives, have poor money management skills, and only open their hearts to dogs and cats.

Seriously, take a good look at your current relationships with your friends, family, coworkers and neighbors. What types of people have you allowed into your life? Are they mature and trustworthy? How do you feel when you are around these people? Which category below is the best fit?

- Do your relationships tend to suck your energy like a vampire? Do you consistently feel drained after talking or being with most of the people in your life? If yes, these are not healthy relationships. You are not doing yourself any favors by allowing their negativity to affect you and drag you down. It can be difficult to distance yourself from them, especially if these people are dependent on your friendship. But if you are trying to become a more positive and healthy person, it is crucial to surround yourself with like-minded people.

- Do your relationships tend to fall into a give-and-take category? For example, is the relationship pleasant and equal in a "this for that" sort of way? When they are down, you lift them. When you are down, they make you smile. Each person takes turns being dependent. And likewise, you feed off each other's joy during happy times. This is an example of a healthy, balanced relationship.

- Do your relationships build your energy up so that you feel like a rocket launching? If yes, fantastic! These types of people are significant and influential in your life and your quest for personal growth. They lift you up and give you a glimpse of how good you can feel.

Where do most of *your* relationships fall? A great formula would be as follows: Obviously you want to release any vampires you may have in your life. Most of your relationships should fall in the give-and-take category. And hopefully, you have one or two rockets in your life.

### Dealing With Breakups

See the good in breakups, or as I call it, relationship clarification. If you realize that the other person is not right for you in the long run, there is no reason to prolong the relationship in its current form. Changing it will open the doors for new opportunities.

Ultimately getting what you want involves learning lessons along the way. Do not view a breakup as a failure. The main reason most people don't move forward in getting what they want is because they are afraid to fail. Realizing something is not working, and then trying something different, is the way to succeed! Think back on the fond memories and honor what you learned from the relationship. These lessons will help you to find a better personality fit next time.

**Already in a Relationship?**

Is your relationship thriving or surviving? Those who are in thriving relationships clearly know what they want out of the relationship, and will not settle for anything less. They know what is most important, such as having a partner with integrity, maturity, and a quest for personal growth.

Relationships need frequent attention and maintenance. Find something new and amazing about your spouse or significant other every day. Think about all the reasons you love them. How does this make you feel? Tell them all the reasons you love them. Focus on their strengths, and help them to grow as a person. Don't take them for granted!

# 48. Progressive Muscle Relaxation

*All is well. You did not come here to fix a broken world.*
*The world is not broken. You came here to live a wonderful life.*
*And if you can learn to relax a little and let it all in, you will begin*
*to see the Universe present you with all that you have asked for.*
— **Abraham Hicks**

What is progressive muscle relaxation?" you may ask. It's a great way to manage stress, relax, and feel centered. The first step is to find a comfortable position. Wear comfortable clothing and prepare your environment so you will not have distractions (be sure to turn off your phone). If your main focus is to use this as a general stress management technique, practice sitting up while you do it. On the other hand, if your goal is to relax your body and mind before falling asleep, try the technique while lying down at bedtime.

Allow conscious relaxation of each body part. Start with your feet,

then lower legs, knees, upper legs, pelvis, abdomen and lower back, chest, and shoulders, relaxing the muscles all the way up your body. As you move up to the head, relax the muscles of your neck, lower jaw, upper jaw, cheeks, eyes, and forehead. Stay focused on any given area until you feel the release of muscle tension.

If you find it difficult to relax a certain area, try tightening the area as much as comfortably possible, creating tension for five to ten seconds before letting go. Repeat this cycle if you still feel tension in that area.

If your mind starts to wander, redirect your attention back to the process, focusing again on your muscles, breathing, and staying calm. Breathe in healing white light and breathe out the stress you have been holding in your body.

Notice areas of tension and pay attention to the mind-body connection. For example, achy knees or hips may make it difficult or uncomfortable for you to move forward physically. Is there a situation in your life that is causing you hesitation about moving forward? If you're experiencing tightness around your eye muscles or problems with your vision, is there a situation in front of you that you don't want to see?

Performing progressive muscle relaxation in a comfortable environment is an excellent practice for use in stressful everyday situations. You can incorporate this technique into your bag of tricks to stay calm and centered as difficult situations arise. When feeling stressed, do a quick scan of your body to see where you are holding tension. Then focus on that area and release it.

If you enjoy meditation, progressive muscle relaxation is a great first step for relaxing the body before working on the mind and spirit.

# 49. The Art of Meditation

*Silence is the great teacher, and to learn its lessons you must pay attention to it. There is no substitute for the creative inspiration, knowledge, and stability that come from knowing how to contact your core of inner silence. The great Sufi poet Rumi wrote, "Only let the moving waters calm down, and the sun and moon will be reflected on the surface of your being."*
— **Deepak Chopra**

Meditation is the practice of raising one's quality of spiritual awareness. The process involves tuning out mental clutter, allowing intuition with yourself and your surrounding world. Meditation is important because it provides a wonderful balance to our busy lives. It brings rest to the body, clarity to the mind, and recharges the spirit. Life coach Alden Witte explains that, as young children, we learn to act in certain ways. For the most part, we now believe that we *are* the acts we learned so long ago.

Meditation is a wakeup call to the realization that at a core level, your ego, patterns, and even some aspects of your personality are not who you really are. Your actions and reactions are learned behaviors that have suited you in the past but may no longer serve you. Meditation can help you get out of your patterns, your rut, to explore new aspects of your personality.

For the most effective technique, find a comfortable way to sit up straight. This is very important for maintaining peak awareness. Meditating while lying down will make it much more difficult to stay focused during the process. If you find that you want to lie down, it may mean that you are resisting the next step in your growth.

Be careful not to get caught up in the dialogue in your head. Make your intention to simply *stop* thinking about things for a few minutes. Focus on clearing your mind, and pay attention to your breathing. The most important thing to remember during your meditation (and any other time) is to be okay with whatever happens.

Practice this process of clearing your mind and focusing on your breathing for just a few minutes a day at first. If you find it helpful, you can extend the length of time for more intense personal growth.

# 50. Never Stop Dancing

*When you dance, your purpose is not to get to a certain place*
*on the floor. It's to enjoy each step along the way.*
— **Wayne Dyer**

What is your attitude about getting older? Do you imagine yourself withering away as you age? Or do you imagine that life just keeps getting better and better with every passing birthday? Attitude is the key! If you imagine that all the good years are gone and it's only downhill from here, it will likely become a self-fulfilling prophecy. If you believe and intend for life to keep improving with age, you will likely be motivated to take good care of yourself, both physically and mentally.

A wonderful inspiration for graceful aging is my grandpa. He is 94 years old, and walks the Cooper River Bridge in Charleston, South Carolina, every year with his family. This event is a steep ten kilometer (just over six miles) walk/run that occurs at the beginning of April, right when the gorgeous azaleas are in full bloom. Grandpa walks almost every day, and goes to the gym to keep himself in shape for this event.

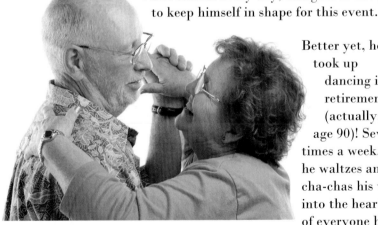

Better yet, he took up dancing in his retirement (actually, at age 90)! Several times a week, he waltzes and cha-chas his way into the hearts of everyone he meets. He even taught me how to do the tango before his 92nd birthday celebration so we could dance together to his favorite song.

In addition to taking care of himself, he shows appreciation for and enriches the lives of those around him. Once I went to visit him for a few days during the middle of the week. "Oh good," he said, "You'll be here on a Wednesday to join my favorite dance group." I was happy to go since he talked about this group so often, and he loves to show off his grandkids. Upon arrival, I was practically carded for being younger than 80 years old!

Grandpa introduced me to the couple who organizes the dance each week. They were elderly, and had danced together all their lives. Unfortunately, the gentleman was no longer able to dance, as he was confined to a wheelchair. So he was the disk jockey. His wife was a great dancer.

A few months later, it was the couple's anniversary. Now, Grandpa's skills don't stop at dancing — he is quite an excellent painter, as well. This was a hobby he took up upon retirement, several decades ago. As a gift to his friends, he had secretly painted an oil portrait of them dancing. Then he asked for all the dancers to bring food that day. It turned into a huge celebration, with lots of delicious dishes, dancing, and fun. When Grandpa presented the painting to the couple, there wasn't a dry eye in the room.

Expect life to get more and more amazing with each day, month and year. Make a New Year's resolution or birthday wish that the coming year is more incredible than the last. Once you establish this goal, brainstorm ways to ensure it becomes the truth. Update your list of things to do during your lifetime. Take that class you've always wanted to take. Explore anew or revisit a hobby or activity you've put on the back burner. Be a little selfish to make sure you are taking care of YOU.

# 51. Attitude and Gratitude

*Our attitudes control our lives. Attitudes are a secret*
*power working twenty-four hours a day, for good or bad.*
*It is of paramount importance that we know*
*how to harness and control this great force.*
— **Tom Blandi**

I have found that the people who are the most content are those who are truly grateful for what they have. We all have different physical characteristics, talents, abilities, and levels of natural intelligence. And we all face challenges and obstacles in our lives. I remember reading that in study after study, those who expressed daily gratitude were happier. This can happen in the form of speaking with another person, prayer, or simply reviewing the day to recall all the wonderful moments for which you are grateful.

Once, though, a friend of mine was in a funk. She was bemoaning the fact that she was overweight, had no chance of getting into an Ivy League school, and her boyfriend had just dumped her. I pointed out to her that while she was overweight, she was also very beautiful and a natural athlete. She might not be going to an Ivy League school, but she loved children and had been accepted at the state teacher's college. While her boyfriend  was no longer on the scene, she was surrounded by a loving family and numerous friends. And of course, now the door was open for her to meet someone even more wonderful. She had so many things to be grateful for, but chose instead to concentrate on the things that brought her down.

We, as humans, have a tendency to think, "I'll be happy when . . . (insert your own situation here)." When what?? Will you be happy when you get a certain job? Earn a million dollars? Graduate from school? Meet your soul mate? Have a family? Buy a home?

Whenever you have achieved something you've wanted in the past, did that achievement cross you over the threshold to eternal happiness? I would venture to say, probably not. Chances are good that you just moved on, focusing your attention on the next thing you believed would become your panacea for Happily Ever After. The cycle continues to repeat itself, but the elusive goal of happiness is never achieved. The reason is that most external sources, such as the abovementioned examples, offer only illusions of happiness. Nothing, I repeat, nothing that is external to you will bring you happiness. As we've already explored, most happiness comes from the profound act of feeling grateful.

Do you appreciate the fact that you can breathe easily? Move your legs to walk? Have the ability to speak? The person who taught me to appreciate every aspect of life is a very memorable patient, Scott Johnson.

Before he came to see me as a first-time patient, I studied Scott's medical chart to learn about his history. During our interaction, he filled me in on the details in answer to my remaining questions. I was surprised that he seemed to downplay his journey until I realized that it didn't matter to him anymore. He had been given a golden ticket for a second chance at life.

Scott, who has given me permission to share his story, was born with cystic fibrosis, a rare genetic disease. Cystic fibrosis affects the lungs and digestive system. It causes the body to produce thick mucus that clogs the lungs and prevents the pancreas from producing the enzymes needed to digest food. The average lifespan for someone with this disease is about 37. There is no cure.

Scott was diagnosed at the age of two months when he was admitted to the hospital for pneumonia and a collapsed lung. Growing up, he was embarrassed about his constant medical needs and incessant coughing. His disease played a major role in his childhood because "people with cystic fibrosis don't think about their future."

When Scott was in his late 20s, he became very sick. An oxygen machine helped him breathe, and he was frequently admitted to the hospital for infections. He lost a tremendous amount of weight, dropping down to just 95 pounds. Scott became sicker and sicker, and was admitted to the hospital yet again. He was told that had about a week to live.

Hospice was called in to provide medical care and services to Scott and his family as his death drew near. The only thing that could save him was a double lung transplant. On his deathbed, Scott made a list of all of the things that he wanted to do if he could only live. The number one item on his list was to complete a triathlon.

A pair of lungs compatible with Scott's blood type and genetic makeup became available several days later. He underwent transplant surgery and received the healthy lungs. The recovery was slow, and was shadowed by the constant fear that his body might reject the new lungs. But he consistently took his anti-rejection medications which suppressed his immune system, making organ rejection less likely. The problem was this medication also made it more difficult for him to fight off illness. Nevertheless, he continued to improve. While his cystic fibrosis was not cured by the transplant, Scott rejoiced at his chance for a longer, healthier life.

As he gained strength, Scott remembered his deathbed dream list. He started out by working with physical therapists and simply learning how to walk again, after lying in a hospital bed for months. The walking led to swimming and biking, and eventually, running. As his strength built, he went on to complete in his first triathlon. His number one "if I could just live" item came true! Then he completed another one. And another. After more triathlons than I can count, he went on to compete in an Ironman event.

Personally, I don't know anyone who has ever attempted this, much less a double-lung transplant recipient with cystic fibrosis. The Ironman Triathlon involves a 2.4-mile swim and a 112-mile bike ride, followed by a 26.2-mile run (marathon).

*Scott Johnson is the only transplant recipient in the world to complete an Ironman competition. He states, "I have cystic fibrosis, but it doesn't have me."*

He is such an inspiration and a wonderful reminder to us all. Why should we wait until our deathbed to have a wake-up call? It's time stop existing and start living!

# 52. The Wooden Cake

*Laughter is an instant vacation.*
— **Milton Berle**

L astly, and probably most importantly, find amusement in
life and surround yourself with people with whom you can
laugh. Spend time with people who don't always take life so
seriously. Have you ever laughed so hard that it was
difficult to breathe, and it felt like you'd just done a million sit-ups?
What a wonderful feeling!

I'll never forget my mom's 60th birthday and the practical joke we
kids played on her. We still can't tell the story without breaking into
uncontrollable laughter. I met my older brother at mom's house on

the afternoon of the big
event. We had secretly
gone to the store and
bought some icing and
lime wedges to decorate
the practical joke —
literally a round wooden
cake. A new recipe, a
lime cake, we decided,
instead of the
traditional key lime pie
Mom loved so much.

We decorated the "cake" beautifully with thick, lime icing and lime
wedges. Then we hid the masterpiece in the laundry room and
waited for her to come home for dinner.

In the meantime, our younger brother (and accomplice) called Mom
to say he was stuck on the military base and wouldn't be home until
late, but not to eat dessert after dinner because he was bringing
something special. "Michael making dessert?" Mom questioned. This
is the kid who usually cooks nothing but meat and potatoes.

After dinner, we sat around the kitchen table talking. It was getting
later and later, and by about 10:30, Mom declared that this dessert
had better be good because she was getting tired! At around 11

p.m., Michael finally came home. We asked mom to leave the room while we prepared the dessert. After pulling the cake from the laundry room and inserting trick candles into the icing, we called her back into the room and sang *Happy Birthday*. She exclaimed, "How beautiful! Let me get the camera!"

As she left the room, my older brother mumbled under his breath, "*Wood burns.*" The trick candles sparkled about. Finally she returned and took forever to set up the camera, as she knew that we would tease her about being a graduate of the Henry XIII School of Photography if she chopped off our heads in the picture.

We naturally handed her the knife for the honor of cutting the first piece. As anticipated, she had trouble cutting into the cake. "Try again," Michael said, "I think the top was a little brown." So she tried again. And again. And again. By this point we were all laughing so hard it was difficult to speak.

I kept the gag going, next asking Michael if he followed the regular or the high-altitude directions. "The regular, I think," he replied easily. "What ingredients did you use?" Mom inquired. Michael went deep into thought, elongating every word: "Eggs, flour, sugar, vanilla . . ." I was pretty impressed with his answer, considering that if it had been me, I think I might have just blurted, "Cake mix."

I asked if I could try to help her cut the cake. Knowing that the wood was actually two round pieces glued together, I found the slot between the two pieces of wood and sliced right into it. "See, it's soft in the middle!" I declared, and handed the knife back to mom. Of course she tried again and couldn't cut it.

After about half an hour, mom finally stated, laughing, "We just can't eat this cake." By then she realized that we had something up our sleeve, so I went into the refrigerator and pulled out a *real* key lime pie for us to enjoy.

Hopefully your family and friends share funny moments like this, too. Take a close look at the people surrounding you. Make a conscious effort to allow only the highest quality people into your life. With this intent and decision, negative people and those who do not contribute to your personal growth will likely just fade away. Do not be saddened or surprised when this happens. It will allow room for new friends and mentors, who are on your same body-mind-spirit path, to enter and shape your positive new journey. So smile big, take a deep breath allowing healing white light into your body, and repeat after me:

> *I pledge allegiance to my health, in honor of my body, mind and spirit. And to my well-being, for which it stands, one life, in this Universe, visibly, with inner peace, health and wellness for all.*

# From the Author

The idea for *Pearls of Wellness* developed from my deep desire to improve the health of my patients by addressing stress and emotions. I noticed in my clinical practice that individuals who experienced frequent illness and disease were often stressed and unhappy. Upon this realization, I began getting to know my patients from a more holistic standpoint. Not only would I address their reasons for their visits, but I would ask about what else was happening in their lives. This gave my patients permission to open up and share their fears, stresses, and joys with me, which enabled me to help them on a much deeper level.

Eventually, I left clinical practice to teach future healthcare providers how to fully connect with their patients. This way, instead of reaching only a limited number of people on any given day, I could reach others exponentially through my students. *Pearls of Wellness* stems from my sincere desire to touch lives by preventing and treating illness from a body-mind-spirit perspective.

# About Laura

Dr. Laura Bank received her clinical education at the Medical University of South Carolina. She practiced medicine as a physician assistant in beautiful, coastal North Carolina. Her specialties included counseling in health optimization, stress management, and weight loss.

She completed a Ph.D. in Health Sciences, which ultimately led to a successful teaching and administration career. Currently, she is the associate program director at A.T. Still University, Arizona School of Health Sciences Physician Assistant Program.

Laura's love of teaching naturally progressed into writing and speaking. Her goal is to touch lives by providing the tools for building healthy lifestyles. She is dedicated to educating people about the powerful body-mind-spirit connection and its effect on overall wellness.

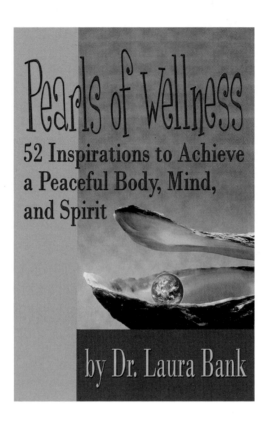

# Pearls of Wellness

52 Inspirations to Achieve a Peaceful
Body, Mind, and Spirit

by Dr. Laura Bank

ISBN:
9780981650708

---

Can't find this book at your local bookstore?

Order:
- Online at www.PearlsOfWellness.com
- By phone at 800-345-6665